☞ W9-CPG-429

08/24
STRAND PRICE
$ 7.00

On Distant Shores

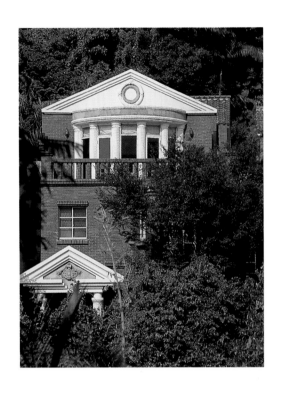

On Distant Shores
Colonial Houses around the World

Ovidio Guaita

The Monacelli Press

First published in the United States of America
in 1999 by
The Monacelli Press, Inc.
10 East 92nd Street, New York, New York 10128.

Copyright © 1999 Leonardo Arte S.r.L., Milan
English edition copyright © 1999
The Monacelli Press, Inc.

All rights reserved under International and Pan-American Copyright Conventions. No part of this book may be reproduced or utilized in any form or by any means, electronic or mechanical, including photocopying, recording, or by any information storage and retrieval system, without permission in writing from the publisher. Inquiries should be sent to The Monacelli Press, Inc.

Library of Congress Cataloging-in-Publication Data
Guaita, Ovidio.
[Villa coloniale. English]
On distant shores : colonial houses around the world / Ovidio Guaita.
p. cm.
Includes bibliographical references.
ISBN 1-58093-051-4
1. Architecture, Colonial. 2. Architecture, Domestic.
3. Architecture, Colonial Pictorial works.
4. Architecture, Domestic Pictorial Works. I. Title.
NA7125.G8313 1999
720'.9—dc21   99-39552

Translated from the Italian by Christopher Evans

Printed and bound in Italy

The author would like to acknowledge the following airlines, tour operators, tourist boards, and others who have furnished indispensible logistical and organizational support:

Alpitour
Il Tucano

United Airlines
Gulf Air

Air France
Air New Zealand
Sayed Mohamad Albukhary, Kuala Lumpur
Australian Tourism Board
Barbados Tourism Authority
Bermuda Tourism/P&DP
Caravan Travel & Tour Agency, Addis Ababa
Ceylon Tourist Board
Corporación de Turismo de Venezuela
Cuba Tourism Office
Curaçao Toeristenbureau
Cyprus National Tourist Board
Danho Daoud, Minister of Tourism Syrian Arab Republic, Damascus
Délégation du Québec
Department of Tourism of Antigua and Barbuda
French National Tourist Board
Pasquale Giorgio, Consolate of Tanzania, Milan
Grace Executive Tourism, Milan
Giuliano Paolo Greco, Gulf Air, Rome
Sian Griffiths, The Peninsula, Hong Kong
Brian Hammond, Sergat, Rome
Hill & Knowlton International, Milan
Hong Kong Tourist Association
Indian National Tourism Agency
Indonesia Tourist Promotion Office
Interazione, Rome
Jamaica Tourism Board
Korean National Tourist Board

Marco Livadiotti, U.T.&T. Sanaa
Macau Government Tourist Office
Malta National Tourist Board
Mauritius Government Tourist Office
Mexican National Tourist Board
Ministry of Tourism of Zanzibar
New Zealand Tourism Board
Office Départemental du Tourisme de la Guadaloupe
Office Départemental du Tourisme de la Martinique
Portugal Tourism Office
Puerto Rico Tourism Company
Seychelles Tourist Office
Singapore Tourism Board
South African Tourism Board
Taipei Cultural and Economic Office
Thailand National Tourist Board
Thema Nuovi Mondi, Milan
Tourism and Industrial Development Company of Trinidad & Tobago

Photograph Credits
All photographs by Ovidio Guaita with the exception of:
page 25 top: Lawrence Taylor
page 341 top and center:
Archivio fotografico F.lli Alinari, Firenze

Most of the drawings were executed by students enrolled in the seminar "The Facade of the Villa" taught by Ovidio Guaita in 1997–98 at the School of Architecture at the University of Florence: Massimiliano Battaglia, Leonardo Bertini, Elena Cupini, Alessandro Cucciarelli, Gianrico Cerri, Alessandro Murgia.

Contents

Houses and Colonies

The San Patricio hacienda *at Latacunga, in Ecuador, an example of British architecture transplanted to the foot of Cotopaxi.*

Opposite:
The spires of an unusual residence among the hills of Venezuela. The exposed wooden structure recalls the architecture of Normandy; the landscape is also similar.

The great age of navigation was followed by the great age of adventure. Travelers, pirates, mercenaries, missionaries, soldiers, and merchants left Europe out of necessity or were driven by a passion for discovery. In the early days of European settlement, the colonists and indigenous peoples coexisted in relative peace, and it was from the native inhabitants that the colonists learned about local lands, resources, cultural traditions, and building methods.

Though colonists initially adopted an indigenous way of life, they gradually started to settle more permanently, employing their own techniques and attempting to re-create the usages and customs of their homelands. Combined with a continual influx of new colonists, the importation of foreign traditions undermined relations with the native inhabitants and led to a period marked by revolts and their bloody suppression, treaties that were regularly disregarded, and forced submission.

The colonists who remained became permanent inhabitants who needed comfortable homes able to accommodate an entire family and represent its status. The residences served as visual, organizational, and social points of reference—marks of ownership. The culture that developed in such places was a mixture, a compromise with the indigenous way of life, with the climate, the latitude and longitude, the spirit of the place. Likewise, colonial architecture is a fusion, made up of forms exported from a hegemonic state and superimposed on the existing ones of a conquered territory. It is therefore the product of two kinds of architecture that coexist and blend, giving rise to a formal, decorative, and extremely heterogeneous syncretism. Thus, for example, wide verandahs were added to austere European structures while *ke-lao* porches of Portuguese inspiration were grafted onto the architecture of Canton and Melaka.

The era of European colonization may be divided into two distinct stages. The first commenced with the voyages of Columbus and the establishment of the Spanish viceroyalties. First Cortés in Mexico and then Pizarro in Peru found fabulous riches and advanced civilizations. News of these discoveries triggered a flow of immigrants from Spain as well as from the Caribbean islands that had already been conquered. A series of commercial bases were founded—Cartagena, Veracruz, Havana, San Juan de Puerto Rico—where Spanish ships landed with cargoes of arms and soldiers and left laden with precious metals. In 1565 the Spanish established a settlement in the Philippines, using the islands as a staging post for silver mined in South America, which served to pay for silk bought in China and shipped to Europe. New cities born in "Nueva España" in this period were dominated by the plateresque style, but the seventeenth century saw the diffusion of Hispano-American baroque, followed by rococo and, at the end of the eighteenth century, neoclassicism.

In the middle of the sixteenth century Portugal consolidated its hold on Brazil, establishing sugarcane plantations and building sugar refineries based on earlier experience at São Tomé in the Gulf of Guinea. In the seventeenth century the coastal belt of Bahia was the principal producer of sugar. In this time of great prosperity Portuguese architecture in Brazil was inspired by models from the homeland, most particularly the Manueline style. At the same time, Northern Europeans (Dutch, English, and French)—who had for a long time plundered the Spanish and Portuguese ships plying the Antilles—turned their pirate lairs on the Caribbean islands into official colonies, establishing legal trade links. Their attitude was more mercantile than colonial; in fact, central governments chose to be represented by joint-stock companies.

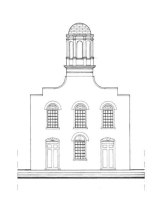

Right:
A little castle with spire-roofed corner towers, at Montego Bay on Jamaica.

Far right:
A unusual circular tower-belvedere atop an early-twentieth-century house in Florida.

Surviving house from the brief period the Dutch occupied Madeira. Although the island's architecture takes its inspiration chiefly from Portugal, a few of the homes built by the Northern European settlers still survive.

Nineteenth-century colonial residence, once belonging to the owner of a tobacco plantation. The large drum brings light into the reception room.

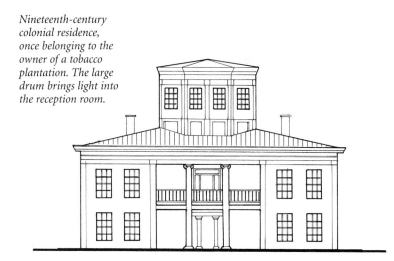

Small house in the Punda quarter of Willemstad, on Curaçao. Formerly the residence of a merchant who arrived in Willemstad before the Dutch, the structure is Portuguese in style.

The Spanish loosened their grip on the Caribbean in the middle of the sixteenth century. At the same time, gold was discovered in Brazil, the importance of sugarcane as a crop declined, and a substantial portion of available resources was diverted into the new mines. The Lesser Antilles—recently established English, French, and Dutch colonies—inherited the production of sugarcane. Curaçao, Martinique, Guadalupe, and Barbados were renamed the "sugar islands" and produced considerable wealth, still reflected today in the elegant homes built by plantation owners.

To make profits the colonists needed labor. The unemployed and the imprisoned were recruited to work in the colonies. However, the conflicts between rich whites, poor whites, and native inhabitants grew increasingly bitter, and the colonists turned to Africa, with its ancestral tradition of commerce in labor—actually forced exchange—between different tribes, as well as the enslavement of prisoners of war. In addition, the expansion of Islam in Africa, especially in the sixteenth and seventeenth centuries, had led to the development of the so-called Muslim slave trade. Thus the Portuguese initiated the "Atlantic slave trade" in the sixteenth century: the forced transfer of slaves from the western coasts of Africa to the new colonies in America. At first the slaves were acquired according to the rules of the African market. But the merchants soon found it more profitable to obtain their own slaves, using mercenaries to bring the captives to collection centers, where they were loaded on ships. The establishment of sugarcane plantations on the Caribbean Islands, which became the symbol

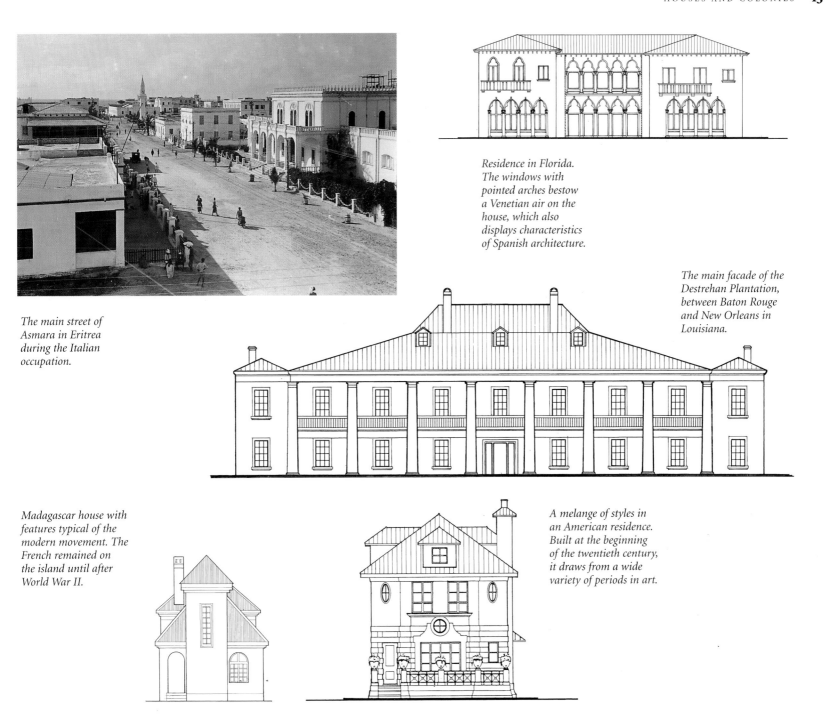

The main street of Asmara in Eritrea during the Italian occupation.

Residence in Florida. The windows with pointed arches bestow a Venetian air on the house, which also displays characteristics of Spanish architecture.

The main facade of the Destrehan Plantation, between Baton Rouge and New Orleans in Louisiana.

Madagascar house with features typical of the modern movement. The French remained on the island until after World War II.

A melange of styles in an American residence. Built at the beginning of the twentieth century, it draws from a wide variety of periods in art.

of European colonization, led to a considerable increase in the traffic in slaves. The same thing was to happen with coffee, cocoa, tobacco, and cotton plantations.

Building typologies in the Caribbean were strongly influenced by the climate. Yet the English traveler Richard Ligon, in the diary he kept during a three-year stay on Barbados (*True and Exact History of the Island of Barbados*, 1657), noted that "the planters never pay attention to the way they build their houses, but just put them up. For this reason many of them are unbearably hot and not even they can spend time inside them without perspiring copiously."

In fact, the high temperature, heavy rain, and high degree of humidity required broad verandahs and large windows, often screened with

jalousies. An alternative was the Demerara window, a design that originally came from Guyana. These were in great demand since they provided effective protection from the sun and rain even when open, thanks to an overhang attached to the upper part of the frame. In addition, the frequency of hurricanes induced people to build horizontally, limiting the height to a single story (which might be raised above the ground to keep out damp and insects). Further south, toward Trinidad, such precautions became less important, since the area was not so subject to the devastating storms.

The principal colonial residences in the Americas were the houses of plantation owners. Before they started to grow such highly profitable crops as sugarcane, the architecture of these buildings was extremely

A house in the Napa Valley of California, in the midst of vineyards.

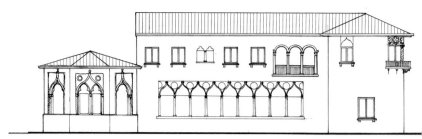

Venetian-style windows on a Spanish-style house in Palm Beach, Florida.

Replica of a Venetian villa to the north of San Francisco in California.

Right:
An imposing American farmhouse. The entrance is marked by a semicircular colonnade with a portico.

Far right:
A typical neo-Palladian pronaos, common in architecture in the eastern United States.

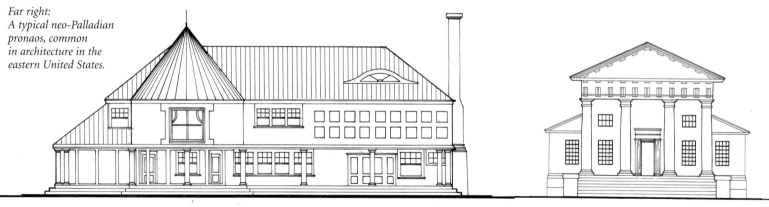

simple. It was only after the colonists acquired an important source of income, and one that required their constant presence, that they decided to build houses that, in spite of the distance, reminded them of their homeland and at the same time symbolized their social standing.

In the British colonies in the Caribbean (Barbados, Antigua, Barbuda, Trinidad and Tobago), the earliest settlements of any architectural significance date from the eighteenth century. The Georgian style exercised a discreet but constant influence, gradually supplanting earlier efforts based on the formal vocabulary of the Middle Ages. (The latter have now vanished, swept away by hurricane and fire.) Different influences prevailed from island to island, so that the style on Barbados can be regarded as almost pure Georgian, while the buildings on Trinidad have distinctly Spanish and French features. In the Lesser Antilles the main construction material was limestone of coral origin: soft, porous, and light, it was easy to work and, since it was locally available in large quantities, inexpensive. The other most common material was wood, also in abundant supply and easy to work. In British colonies, however, its use was restricted to buildings of smaller size and minor importance, since it was considered a humble material.

In 1780 a powerful hurricane swept across much of the Antilles, leaving devastation in its wake. But the profits from the plantations were by then so high that the planters were able to rebuild on a grand scale. It was at this time that a particular style, derived from English traditions but strongly influenced by the sunny climate, spread through the region.

Lawrence Hall in
Lahore, Pakistan.
Built in 1861, it was
for many years the
symbol of British rule.

*The garden front of the
nymphaeum of Villa
Vizcaya, in Miami. It is
a perfect reproduction of
an Italian Renaissance
residence.*

*Two pavilions flanking
the central block of a
Palm Beach mansion.
It was inspired by late-
nineteenth-century
French tradition.*

*The neoclassical
residence of the British
governor in Lahore.*

The style was given the name—by later historians of architecture—of Caribbean Georgian.

Toward the end of the eighteenth century and after the French Revolution, slavery was abolished. For a long time, however, the plantations remained profitable as the freed slaves continued to work: although they were paid, their former owners were no longer obligated to provide for their needs. Yet this development was also the first stage in the decline of the plantations.

The second period of European colonization began in the eighteenth century and was directed toward Asia and Africa, two continents that had hitherto barely been explored, apart from the foundation of a few commercial bases. It was Portugal above all that, instead of setting out to con-quer territory, established trading posts and fortress-markets: the first of these were founded on the east coast of Africa, the northern coasts of the Indian Ocean, and in the Malay archipelago. In all there were about fifty, stretching from Maputo to Goa and on to Hormuz, Melaka, Macau, and even Nagasaki. The British East India Company also maintained a presence in the East, with bases at Madras, Bombay, Calcutta, and Canton. The strongest mercantile force, though, was the Dutch East India Company, which possessed a site of vital commercial importance in the Far East: the port of Batavia (now Jakarta). Its canals were lined with houses featuring the typical rounded pediments of the Dutch baroque, just like those of New Amsterdam (later New York), Oranjestad (on the island of Aruba), and Willemstad (the main town on Curaçao).

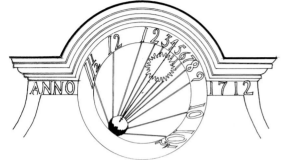

Eighteenth-century sundial on the facade of an Italian-inspired residence.

Corbels and friezes, typical of buildings inspired by classical antiquity. They are modeled in stone or, more often, stucco.

A tower with an onion-shaped dome. Europeans often adopted compositional elements from the Eastern countries they had colonized.

A townhouse on Curaçao. Gables are a Dutch trademark around the world.

At the same time—and in some cases into the twentieth century—the Ottomans, Omanis, Russians, Moguls, Chinese, and Japanese were following their own imperialist traditions. The Ottoman state, consolidated after the capture of Constantinople in 1453, had existed as a political entity since the thirteenth century. In the sixteenth century it became an extraterritorial dynastic empire that extended its rule first over the Balkans and then over the Near East, annexing the Mameluke sultanate and occupying northeast Africa. At the height of Ottoman splendor, in the mid-sixteenth century, its territories were dotted with magnificent urban palaces and townhouses. Relatively austere on the outside, they were opulent and elegant on the inside, filled with courtyards, patios, fountains, and plays of water, and decorated with paintings and mosaics. Another

Islamic sultanate, that of Oman, even shifted its capital from Muscat to Zanzibar to underline the importance of its overseas territories. China and Japan alternated dominance over neighboring regions, in particular Korea and Formosa, or Taiwan. At times China extended its rule to central Asia (Turkistan) and the Himalayan tableland (Nepal and Tibet).

With the industrial revolution Europe achieved a technological dominance that allowed it to establish sway over the rest of the world, and in the nineteenth century Europeans left more traces of their passage than in all the preceding centuries, with the sole exception of the Spanish viceroyalties in the New World. The nineteenth century also saw the division of Africa, until 1879 a virtually unexplored land of tribal kingdoms and ancient hunting grounds. As early as 1830 the French had tried to conquer

Hearst Castle in California. The great mansion is one of the most unusual and most fascinating examples of eclectic colonial architecture.

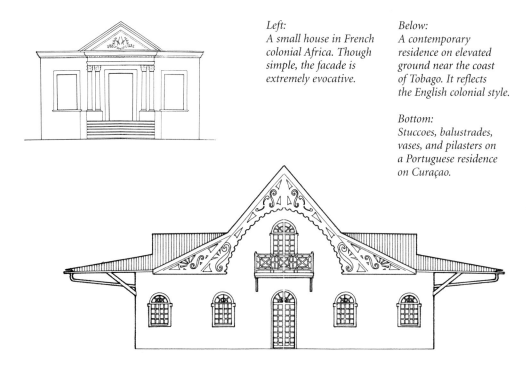

Left:
A small house in French colonial Africa. Though simple, the facade is extremely evocative.

Below:
A contemporary residence on elevated ground near the coast of Tobago. It reflects the English colonial style.

Bottom:
Stuccoes, balustrades, vases, and pilasters on a Portuguese residence on Curaçao.

Suburban house with wood decoration.

Algeria, and later a series of French and English enclaves was created alongside formerly powerful Portuguese bases. The Conference of Berlin in 1884 was followed by an assault on Africa. Even nations that had previously shown no interest in colonization took part. Germany, for instance, settled Namibia, Tanzania, and Cameroon, while Belgium colonized the Congo and its precious diamond mines. Italy reached Somalia in 1889 and went on to conquer Eritrea, Tripoli, and, for a brief period in the 1930s, Ethiopia.

After World War II, however, the political balance altered drastically, the centers of the worldwide trade in colonial goods shifted, and the fortunes of individual colonies varied greatly. New sectors of production emerged, such as that of bananas, along with new commercial activities.

The great houses of the colonists became expensive and often anachronistic white elephants. Many of the most important of them, dating from the eighteenth and nineteenth centuries, the golden age of the colonies, had been built of perishable materials, and thus began a slow but inexorable decline.

Symbols of a culture that for good or ill characterized an era, the colonists' homes survive today as testimony to a phase in human history founded on contrasting values and often deplorable modes of conduct. They are an expression of vanished ways of life, of nostalgia for the past, of brutality. They are also symbols of the human spirit of discovery; of inventiveness, versatility, and adaptability; and of a thirst for knowledge and achievement.

Great Britain came late to colonial power. The British East India Company was unable to compete with its Dutch counterpart, and its territories in the New World were initially confined to the thirteen colonies strung out from the peninsula of Newfoundland to the border with Florida. The rest of North America belonged to France and Spain.

It was only in the nineteenth century, after the definitive loss of many of its possessions in America, that the focus of British interests shifted to the East, and to India in particular. By 1805 trade with the Indian subcontinent was already firmly in the hands of the British crown, and in 1858 the country was placed under direct British administration, making India the hub of the colonial empire. From India the British went on to Malaysia, Australia, and New Zealand, setting up protectorates all over the East.

The buildings they constructed in these territories were in the Victorian style of architecture, named after the long-lived and resolute queen. The Gothic, Renaissance, and baroque elements of this style, combined with the tropical climate, gave rise to an extraordinary kaleidoscope of forms.

A Merry-Go-Round of Styles

In the middle of the eighteenth century there were thirteen British colonies in America. Known as chartered colonies—they were founded on the basis of concessions granted by special charters—they were all to some extent dependent on the British crown. The first to be given official status was Virginia, set up by independent British settlers who had moved there to cultivate and process tobacco.

The styles of architecture in the colonies were extremely varied. At the outset Jacobean had the upper hand. This was an extremely simple style, derived from the English architecture of the Middle Ages. It was soon enriched by Renaissance elements, giving rise to a hybrid known as Georgian, a more opulent and varied style that is conventionally divided into three periods, Early, High, and Late. It remained popular even after the revolution of 1776, as an "Americanized" version of the neo-Palladianism that was proving a great success in Britain.

The large pronaoi characteristic of this style were most widely used in the center and south of the United States, where the climate was milder. Such forms even proved popular in the former French colonies, such as Louisiana, where they were favored by an existing propensity toward classicism. In these houses the Palladian concept of a correspondence between form and function, and between architecture and landscape, prevailed. The next style to emerge was the Federal, also known as Neoclassical. Typical of the first half of the nineteenth century, it stemmed from the great success that neoclassicism had had in Europe.

After the Civil War, the spread of neo-Palladianism and all things connected with classicism was brought to a halt until the emergence of the Colonial Revival at the end of the century. This half-hearted return to the stylistic features of classicism was followed by innovations inspired by the Ecole des Beaux-Arts, which were characterized by a refined and decidedly more complex manner that was to clear the way for an increasingly original approach to architecture.

Preceding pages:
Villa Escudero, in the
vicinity of Manila.

Below:
Wrought-iron gate at the
entrance to a stately
home in Williamsburg,
Virginia.

The elegant facade
of Thomas Jefferson's
Monticello, near
Charlottesville. Set
in one of Virginia's lush
parks, the estate was
long regarded as a
model of agricultural
organization.

The riverfront entrance of Westover Plantation in Virginia. Its Georgian facade is characterized by the use of unplastered brick as a decorative motif.

The Elms at Newport, Rhode Island. The neoclassical residence stands on Atlantic Avenue, a road lined with great mansions.

The main front of Westbury Hall, Los Angeles. Covered with ivy, it blends in well with the architecture and plays an important part in the overall impression of the building.

One of the bedrooms at Shirley Plantation in Virginia. The house, which dates from the first half of the eighteenth century, still belongs to the family of tobacco planters who had it built.

Rosecliff Hall at Newport, Rhode Island. It was designed in an elegant neoclassical style.

The long drive, lined with topiary evergreen bushes, leading to Crossways House. Another enchanting residence in Newport, it is a successful late example of the transplantation of neo-Palladianism to the New World.

The imposing
semicircular portico of
a suburban mansion
in Memphis, Tennessee.
The combination of
brick and stone provides
the decoration of the
main facade.

A private garden in
Albuquerque, New
Mexico. The Romantic
style is reminiscent
of Hyde Park or the
Bois de Boulogne.

Guenoc farmhouse, in the Napa Valley to the north of San Francisco. Famous for its excellent wines, the region is dotted with elegant residences built from the nineteenth century onward.

Porch around Guenoc farmhouse. Built of wood, it faces carefully tended vineyards.

Wood and brick in the colonial residences of past and present. Southernmost House lends a touch of colonial-Caribbean atmosphere to Key West.

Key West, the last of Florida's islands. Just a stone's throw from Cuba, it has long been one of America's favorite vacation resorts.

Houses on Key West. Tall and narrow or low and wide, the structures on Key West are built mostly out of wood in a relaxed and informal style.

*Left:
Colonial house built
of wood in Petaluma,
California.*

*Below:
Residence in Calistoga,
California. The original
settlers of California's
Napa Valley were
primarily from Ireland
and Great Britain.*

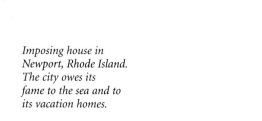

*Imposing house in
Newport, Rhode Island.
The city owes its
fame to the sea and to
its vacation homes.*

Waterfront house in Florida. At the turn of the century, the state became the vacation spot of choice, particularly Miami, Palm Beach, and Key West. The state capital, Tallahassee, has numerous waterside homes built in styles that show the influence of Central and South America.

Southway, Palm Beach. Stately and neoclassical houses are characteristic of the area.

The garden front of Valverde villa in Santa Barbara, California. The small city is filled with the sumptuous homes of stars from the world of entertainment.

Right and far right: Details of structures in the garden surrounding Filioli House in San Francisco.

In the Shade of Limestone

It is no accident that Bermuda has long been considered one of the most beautiful places in the world. So small and yet so varied, it is replete with charming creeks, wonderful beaches, lush vegetation, and ever-changing panoramas. Settled for the first time in 1609 by adventurers on their way to Virginia to set up tobacco plantations, Bermuda is still a colony of the British Crown, though a self-governing one. Strategically located on the route between England and North America, it has never experienced a decline.

The lack of hostility on the part of the island's native inhabitants encouraged the colonists to settle and to construct substantial buildings. The most widely used material was limestone, not a particularly resistant or beautiful stone in comparison with the stone of the Old World, but one that was combined in Bermuda with boldly colored walls to produce a rather tropical effect. When quarried the limestone is white in color, but it tends to turn gray on exposure to atmospheric agents. The stone was used along with cedar wood, which was not very plentiful but was sturdy and reliable.

Some of the dwellings are hybrid affairs, halfway between the vernacular tradition and the Victorian style, while others look like country manor houses and a few even show neo-Gothic influences. At first it was common to place pronaoi at the entrances, but then taste shifted toward the Georgian style, imported from the nearby British colonies in North America. Wherever possible, houses were built facing the sea and given fairly complex plans (in the shape of an X, L, H, T, or U), including wings at the sides. In many cases, however, they were only a single room deep to promote ventilation.

In *The Tempest* Shakespeare celebrated the newly discovered island of Bermuda as a paradise on earth. Over the centuries it has served as a refuge for politicians, magnates, adventurers, and artists, many of whom built homes there. Large or small, these constructions have always served as status symbols.

Camden House, now open to the public. It is one of the best-known eighteenth-century mansions in the Georgian style on Bermuda. The interiors still have the original furniture, which was shipped from London.

The main facade of Camden House. Conceding little to British tradition, it is faced with airy balconies. The building is now the official residence of the prime minister.

*Playful details on a
Bermuda residence.
Styles on the island are
often combined freely.*

*Pastel colors and fanciful
moldings on a Bermuda
house. Styles are blended
in free flights of fantasy.*

Bloomfield House, built near Paget at the beginning of the eighteenth century. It is one of Bermuda's best-known mansions. The main front faces onto a lush garden.

Rear facade of Bloomfield House, which opens onto a glade that stretches out to the open fields.

Cambridge Beaches, an upper-class residence converted into a vacation resort. Beautifully restored, it is set into a large park.

Top and above: Interpretations of the original Bermudan style, a blend of European forms and tropical colors.

Mount Pleasant, one of the finest houses on the island. Large and airy, it has a two-story porch along the main front. Recently restored, it is an excellent example of the distinctive fusion of styles that characterizes Bermudan architecture.

Front drive leading to a Bermudan house. Unspoiled nature, pastel colors, and an indigo sky characterize the island.

In the Homes of Planters and Governors

West Indies

Below:
Marine Lodge, built at the beginning of the twentieth century on the outskirts of Bridgetown, Barbados. The wooden main floor stands on an open basement of masonry.

Bottom:
Late-eighteenth-century Harmony Hall in the parish of St. Michael on Barbados. It is one of the island's oldest buildings and was enlarged several times. An open gallery runs along three sides of the house.

White and airy houses of sugarcane planters alternate with imposing residences of governors and wealthy merchants, enriching the West Indies with charming works of architecture. Such dwellings can be found in the Greater Antilles, from Jamaica to the American Cuba of the first half of the century and Puerto Rico, as well as on Antigua, Barbados, and Trinidad and Tobago.

On all of the islands, these noble buildings were intended to house the families of planters or landowners. Coffee, cotton, and sugarcane were the new sources of wealth, and slaves imported from Africa provided the necessary work force. Colonists perceived the new lands as their own and wanted to build grand and comfortable homes on them.

Most of the so-called great houses in which the plantation owners lived were located outside the urban centers. Set in the middle of estates, often of vast size, they were generally built on hilltops so that the inhabitants could enjoy the breeze and view. The houses were characterized by large patios, which served as extensions of the living room, and were built chiefly of wood, the cheapest and most abundant material.

Unlike on the islands where French and Spanish influence was dominant, balconies and verandahs had a private character and were often enclosed by blinds or sunscreens or even relegated to the sides and back of the house. The kitchen and bathroom, on the other hand, were located in small buildings adjacent to but separate from the owner's house. On these islands formerly ruled by Spain, dwellings in the British colonial style acquired details, nuances, and colors typical of Hispanic colonial architecture, resulting in a harmonious and graceful blend.

In addition to lush tropical vegetation and long beaches, famous all over the world, the West Indies offer a number of other attractions, certainly including the architecture. And the residences of Anglo-Saxon inspiration are the perhaps the ones that, with their rigid and rather formal geometry, contrast most strongly with the sensual and exhilarating scenery.

The porch of Greenwood Great House at Montego Bay, Jamaica.

Casa d'Esopo, one of the oldest mansions in San Juan, Puerto Rico. Very few concessions have been made to modern conveniences; the furniture has been handed down for generations.

Rose Hall Great House, set majestically on a rise near Montego Bay, in the northern part of Jamaica. Its architecture, halfway between the baroque and the Neoclassical, makes it unique on the island.

Stolmayer Castle on Trinidad. Battlements, turrets, and spires are set alongside open galleries and large windows, echoing neo-Gothic examples from the Old World.

Mille House on Trinidad. The materials used depended on the financial means of the client.

Vale Royal in Kingston, Jamaica. Long the governor's residence, it is now the official home of the president of the republic.

Top:
A spacious verandah runs along three sides of Clarence House, on Antigua. Its large park allows an unobstructed view of the sea.

Above:
Villa DuPont at Playa Varadero, Cuba. It was built in 1926 by the American Eleuthère Irenée DuPont as a vacation house. The eclectic style combines Moorish balconies, baroque columns (carved out of mahogany), and Art Nouveau elements.

Right:
Royal Westmoreland,
Barbados. Houses in new
areas of development
retain a distinctly
colonial flavor.

Far right:
Francia Plantation, set
in a lush park in the
middle of Barbados.
A flight of steps leads to
the main floor, and a
double portico frames
the entrance.

St. Nicholas Abbey,
Barbados.

*House on Tobago.
Though recently
built, the design recalls
colonial precedents.*

*Main facade of the
Tobago house. The
wooden tympanum is
outlined by delicate
arabesques.*

*A house on Trinidad.
The nature is
so luxuriant that it
appears to enfold
every construction.*

*Overleaf:
St. Nicholas Abbey,
Barbados, one of the
earliest sugarcane
plantations on the island.
The structures used to
refine the sugarcane have
their own architectural
characteristics.*

Sam Lord's Castle, in
an isolated spot in the
north of the island of
Barbados. It was built in
1820 and is known for
mahogany columns
and panels and stuccoed
ceilings.

Top:
Clifton Hall, Barbados.
An overhang shelters the
windows from rain.

Above:
Woodland, Barbados.

Royal Vacation Homes

Mediterranean Basin

From the abodes of the Knights of Malta to those of Cyprus, Aphrodite's island, and those of Capri, Rhodes, and Crete, the British established a presence wherever an enchanted isle rose out of the Mediterranean at a strategic location.Sometimes the reason was military or economic, and sometimes simple tourism prevailed.

Owing to its crucial position at the center of the Mediterranean, halfway between the West and the East, Malta has always been a land of contention. It was conquered by the Phoenicians, Romans, Arabs, and Normans in turn. The British arrived at the beginning of the nineteenth century and remained until 1964. The island, though partly arid, is rendered an ideal place for vacations by the year-round mild climate and the abundance of fruit that grows there. The ruins of villas built by the Romans can still be seen at Rabat and Mdina. Later their place was taken by the Knights and then by the colonists.

In the island's architecture Renaissance and baroque forms are blended with an abundance of Arab influences and refined evocations of the Victorian and neoclassical styles. The disparate structures are fused by the ocher of the local mortar used for plastering, made from a special mud of marine origin. The influence of the Anglo-Saxon colonists has been discreet, and its effect on the architecture diluted by the blue expanse of the Mare Nostrum.

While the island of Cyprus is still disputed today, it should not be forgotten that a century of British domination came to an end only in 1964 and followed a much longer period under the Ottoman yoke, though this time was far less significant architecturally. When the prime minister of Great Britain, Lord Beaconsfield, visited the island as a young man, he described it as a "rosy country of Venus, romantic kingdom of the Crusades."

British culture has always owed a great deal to the Mediterranean basin, and the colonies that the country established there served only to strengthen this influence. There was little of the Northern European in the houses the British colonists built: vaguely Arab in style, they were well adapted to the islands' rocky outcrops and suited to a land that has always been a crossroads between Europe, Africa, and Asia.

A two-story portico facing a residential street in Nicosia, Cyprus.

The Auberge de Castille, one of the finest buildings in Valletta. Its immaculate walls recall the baroque townhouses of London, but there were also many Central European influences, due to the varied origins of the Knights of Malta.

The hall of Ta Cénc at Gozo, an eighteenth-century residence built entirely of stone. Now part of an elegant resort, the house offers visitors the chance to stay in an authentic colonial house.

Projecting windows, characteristic of Valletta. Like miniature drawing rooms, they face the main street.

Lugisland, an elegant baroque dwelling in the center of Rabat, Malta. Set behind thick walls, it has an elaborate semicircular staircase leading to the entrance.

A mansion in Rabat where neoclassicism and the Gothic Revival are blended heterogeneously.

Above:
Neoclassical building on
the outskirts of Larnaca,
Cyprus.

Right:
Portico with stone
columns in Nicosia,
Cyprus.

Opposite:
Two-story porch
supported by coupled
columns in the
Maltese hinterland.

Dignified Tropical Ways

Seychelles

A Seychellois house, with the characteristic raised central block, in a contemporary watercolor.

On the Seychelles European planters succeeded in marrying the forms and styles of their homeland to the climate and materials of Africa. Even the most stately of their houses consisted of a main floor set atop storehouses and under a mansard, sometimes reserved for the servants. Wooden beams set on piles, sunk to a depth of about one-and-one-half feet in the ground, formed the supporting structure; the most widely used materials were *capucin,* a hardwood rarely attacked by insects, and the cheaper but less resistant mango, cedar, and casuarina. Roofs were traditionally made out of dried leaves and bound together with ropes of coconut fiber or lianas, but since World War II corrugated iron, often brightly painted in colors inspired by the nature of the archipelago, has become widespread. The interior generally consists of a large living room surrounded by bedrooms. The kitchen is located in a separate building, sometimes linked by a covered passage. The bathroom is always separate and built similarly to the main building.

In the Seychelles the numerous references to European architectural traditions are set in the context of a totally different climate, forcing their reinvention.The result is fascinating, and it is relevant even to those working at quite different latitudes. The efficient arrangement of the rooms, the orientation of the patios, and the insertion of special wooden grills in the walls favor ventilation, providing an effective alternative to artificial air conditioning. The system saves considerable energy and is certainly much more environmentally friendly.

While the beautiful beaches of the Seychelles are world-famous, the architecture is one of the most interesting legacies of the colonial period, and certainly the most evident. From the modest homes of the island natives to the grand residences of the colonists—first the French and then the British—accommodation for the Seychellois is the fruit of painstaking attention to detail and sophisticated technical expedients and offers both brilliant colors and a welcoming atmosphere.

State House, formerly the governor's residence. The style is neoclassical, stately and imposing, and contrasts strongly with the lush vegetation that surrounds it.

Seychelles roof. Often made of corrugated iron laid over a wooden framework, such roofs are enlivened by surprising colors and forms.

Two brightly colored roofs amid the greenery.

St. Joseph House, on the island of Mahé. The typical colonial residence is perfectly adapted to the local climate.

Dwelling to the north of the capital, Victoria. The structure is set in a variegated and lush garden that separates it from the road.

The main floor of Bailey House on Mahé. The verandah, furnished like a living room, fuses interior and exterior.

Residence on La Digue. The construction method is the same one used in the capital, but the materials and details are simpler.

"Out of Africa"

For decades Central Africa, and above all Kenya, attracted Europeans anxious to experience the thrill of a safari on its famous savannah. Quite a few visitors decided to stay, setting up one of the country's numerous farms and living the kind of exhilarating life described by author Karen Blixen (Danish by birth but British by marriage).

It was but a short step from tents to great houses: the abundant supply of wood, labor, and economic resources made life relatively easy for subjects of the British Crown blessed with even the slightest spirit of adventure. Their homes were characterized by large patios, bladed fans, enormous mosquito nets, and adjoining huts for services. Never truly Victorian, they were not really "African" either.

Farther south, between Johannesburg and Cape Town, age-old camphor trees preside over the private realms of some of the most suggestive colonial mansions in southern Africa. All around lie elegant geometric patterns of vineyards and orchards, natural appendages of this little-known area. The enchanting natural scenery of the continent's southern tip forms a backdrop for elegant Victorian architecture, always poised between tradition and innovation.

Stellenbosch, the "city of oaks," is acknowledged to be the capital of the South African wine industry. Founded in 1679 by a group of Dutchmen led by the future governor Simon van der Stel (the city's namesake), it rapidly grew rich and famous on the strength of its vineyards. The settlers, especially those who arrived from Great Britain at the turn of the twentieth century, came from land-owning stock, and their dream was to find an idyllic place where they could live peacefully, surrounded by the beauty of nature.

Today the old farmhouses of the colonial period stand alongside modern houses that hark back to the styles of the past, from Cape Dutch to Regency, Georgian, and Victorian. The result is decidedly eclectic but charming, a worthy architectural setting for the dream of the colonists.

An interior in Kenya, a blend of tribal and Anglo-Saxon traditions.

Northwards House in the center of Johannesburg. The brick and stone building looks as if it were imported from the heart of Yorkshire.

House in Johannesburg.
British and Dutch
influences are both
evident in the
decoration.

Left and far left:
Interior of Melrose
House in Pretoria.
One of the best-known
mansions in the capital,
it used to belong to the
owners of a diamond
mine.

*The verandah of
Ellingham House in
the province of KwaZulu/
Natal, on the coast of
the Indian Ocean. Its
owners run a large
coconut plantation.*

*Turrets, dormer
windows, gables, and
columns on a house
in Pretoria. Only the
surrounding nature
betrays the location.*

House in Pretoria. Unlike Cape Town, characterized by Dutch influences, most of the architecture in the capital is in the British colonial style.

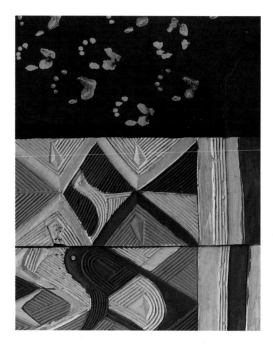

Wall decorated with tribal motifs in Nigeria. Women are chiefly responsible for these embellishments, which are not infrequently combined with forms drawn from European construction traditions.

Mogul Tradition and Victorian Innovation

Indian Subcontinent

The townhouses of Lahore. Built in the eighteenth and nineteenth centuries, the dwellings were celebrated for their splendor and for the art treasures they contained.

In 1498, after Vasco da Gama had opened up a trade route by sea, the Portuguese established the first commercial links with the Indian region. Afterward the Dutch and, in the mid-seventeenth century, the French dominated. The latter, defeated by the British in the middle of the eighteenth century, were forced to withdraw. The efficiency of the British military machine, combined with the decadence of the Mogul empire, played a decisive role in the triumph of Western imperialism in what are now the nations of India and Pakistan.

From Karachi to Lahore and from Delhi to Bombay, formal urban residences coexist with country houses that are more private in character but no less magnificent in appearance. Originally hunting lodges, pavilions for festivities, or vacation homes, these buildings express a desire for grandeur that knew no limits. The forts of Rajasthan are another important architectural inheritance, as are those of Lahore, capital of the Mogul renaissance. The "Pakistani Florence" is still one of the most fascinating cities on the Indian subcontinent, and its numerous residences are a testimony to the glory of the past.

The situation is similar in neighboring Sri Lanka, which under its former name of Ceylon was a base for the spice trade; its history stretches back centuries. Yet the island maintains strong ties with its indigenous traditions and culture. Today its remarkably varied architecture bears witness to the colonial. On the coast from Colombo to Galle is a series of elegant residences characterized by broad porches decorated with lacy woodwork and triangular tympana. Neoclassical buildings alternate with ethereal structures that seem to have been derived from the native huts. Nineteenth- and twentieth-century cottages are found six thousand feet up in Nuwara Eliya.

Nature is a powerful presence on the Indian subcontinent, and one of the most fascinating aspects of the area is the contrast between the tropical setting and the European architecture; typical of many colonies, the juxtaposition is more striking here. The residences of Pakistan, India, and Sri Lanka testify to a period that, notwithstanding its wars and iniquities, has made a decisive contribution to the artistic and architectural history of the region.

A small colonial house at Anuradhapura, in the north of Sri Lanka. An important religious center, the city was also a vacation resort for the functionaries of the British empire.

The vestibule of
Umaid Bhawan Palace
in Jodhpur, Rajasthan.
Built at the beginning of
the twentieth century, it
has recently been turned
into a hotel.

The imposing main
front of the magnificent
Jodhpur palace, seen
from the driveway. One
wing is still occupied by
the maharajah, heir of
the man who built it.

*A view of the hall of
Umaid Bhawan Palace,
one of the most majestic
and solemn of all Indian
private residences. The
impressive dome atop the
hall is visible from the
outside as well.*

Colonial dwelling on Sri Lanka. Porches and verandahs are characteristic of Sri Lanka, especially on the coast between Colombo and Galle, a favored site of British colonists.

House in Nuwara Eliya, high in the central mountains of Sri Lanka. The half-timbering is typical of Northern Europe.

Colonial mansion in Lahore, northern Pakistan.

Oriental eclecticism on the outskirts of Lahore. Mogul and neo-Gothic elements are amalgamated in a mansion.

Left and far left: Architectural niches in Pakistan.

Farmhouse at Derawar
built at the beginning of
the twentieth century,
when large estates were
still in British hands.

Colonial dwelling in
Lahore. In the residential
districts of the city, white
neoclassical buildings
were the preferred style.

House in Shekhūpura,
not far from Lahore.
Many neoclassical
residences located at
crossroads have double
facades so that they can
be admired from both
directions.

*Patio corner in Lahore.
Unplastered brick is used
to decorate the building,
which blends classical
and Georgian motifs.*

*Eclectic balcony facing
the main street of
Multan in the north of
Pakistan. It combines
Victorian elements with
Art Nouveau stylistic
features.*

Colonial-style buildings in Lahore. Many of the structures erected in the city at the turn of the century by the British display a marked Mogul influence.

Fusion of local and imported stylistic elements. Both influences are skillfully juggled in arches, columns, portals, and stairways.

Residence of a high official in a residential district of Lahore.

The Cricket Club in Lahore. Derived from Victorian architecture, it has been "opened up" to improve ventilation.

Baroque Pagodas

Far East

Phra Nakhon Khiri Palace in Phetchaburi province, Thailand. The terrace offers a view of the surrounding dense tropical vegetation.

In Hong Kong, Taiwan, the Philippines, and Thailand, skyscrapers, high technology, and unimaginable luxuries are combined with ancient villages and pleasant royal clubs. Though westerners to some extent shaped the image of this world over centuries of dominion, they were never able to grasp its true soul, and the colonies remained firmly rooted in the culture, religion, and tradition of the East. The only real exception is the fervently Catholic Philippines. Relations with the local population were based on cooperation (whether willing or not), not on integration. The British realized that the area would never become another India and acted accordingly.

Until quite recently, life in this part of the world centered around the family village, a group of houses opening onto a central courtyard: around the fake castles and neoclassical pronaoi of Phuket, which, like the rest of Thailand, was never colonized but absorbed the colonial style nevertheless; around the bright pink fronts of houses in Manila; around the austere Victorian mansions of the well-to-do quarter of Taipei (like Thailand, never a British colony). Although the bourgeois lifestyle has grown ever more widespread, producing stunning blends of elements as disparate as Chinese pagodas and baroque and rococo dwellings, it is the contrast between West and East, between past and future, that remains most fascinating.

Hong Kong—the Peak, the Tiger Balm Garden, a floating restaurant at Aberdeen— is one of the last remnants of Europe in the Far East. The most recent of the colonies to be to be set free after centuries of foreign rule, it too has been a place of exchange and common growth.

Elegant stairway leading to the Phetchaburi palace. The former country residence of the royal family, it was built in the middle of the nineteenth century by King Rama IV.

Douglas Castle in Hong Kong, one of the most enigmatic constructions in the former colony.

A classical citation, revised and corrected, in the royal palace at Phetchaburi, Thailand.

Semicircular portico at the entrance to a mansion in Phuket.

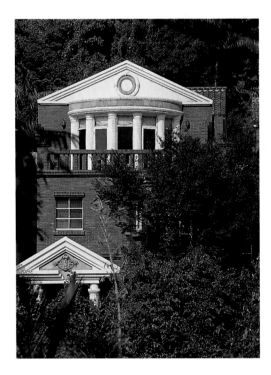

Far left: Neoclassical house in Taipei.

Left: A building on the grounds of the royal palace at Ayutthaya, former capital of Thailand.

Opposite: Colonial residence at Phuket.

Architectural Melting Pot

A projecting window in Singapore. The land's rich forms and colors reflect the many different peoples who have passed through.

Singapore's extraordinary success is due above all to its location at the junction of the main trade routes between East and West. Sir Stamford Raffles, administrator of the East India Company, declared the island a British protectorate in 1819 and drew up the plan of the city. After the arrival of the British, Singapore took over a role previously played by Melaka—international port and trading post that attracted merchants from every nation—and has retained this role ever since. Situated close to the equator, the city-state is known as the "Garden City" and has also been baptized "instant Asia," a place where 2.8 million inhabitants—Chinese, Malay, Indian, and Eurasian—live together while preserving their own traditions, religions, and cuisine in a fascinating melting pot.

Little India, Arab Street, and Chinatown are the names given to some of the areas inhabited by the various ethnic groups within Singapore. They compose a colorful and phantasmagoric world of batiks, temples, "shophouses," fortune-tellers, and teeming markets filled with the odor of spices. A great number of festivals, which follow a whole series of different calendars, transform the streets into improvised stages.

Malaysia, to the north, is characterized by the elegant residences of British and local high society. Thatched or tiled roofs testify to a marriage of two worlds, with their contrasting styles, materials, and customs. Partly out of respect and partly out of a desire to leave dust and mud outside, people remove their shoes before entering Malaysian houses. Only in the residences of the colonists is this practice not followed, and so none of the sandals, slippers, and boots generally seen outside Malay homes rest under the great neoclassical colonnades and on the patios of Victorian houses.

A Corinthian capital atop a pilaster in Singapore. Only the colors betray that it is located in the tropics.

A residence on the island of Penang. Porticos, verandahs, and tympana are the characteristic elements of Malaysian houses.

Carcosa Ser Negara, one of the most important dwellings in Kuala Lumpur, now converted into a hotel.

Two windows of a building in Penang. Some aspects of the city's architecture still show the influence of the Portuguese.

A wrought-iron decoration on the marble wall of a house in Kuala Lumpur.

English homes
transplanted to the
equator. Only a few
traces of traditional
British architecture
survive.

Below and right:
Colonial residences in
Singapore. The walls are
less substantial, pierced
by large expanses of
windows, verandahs,
and blinds.

*Left and below:
Penang residence. The
homes of rubber-
plantation owners and
merchants testify to the
wealth of the island with
elements of classicism—
orders, arches, and
tympana—skillfully
combined with a variety
of elements drawn from
the baroque lexicon.*

*Restored upper-class
home in Penang.*

White classical building amid the green gardens of Johor Baharu, a city in the far south of the peninsula, opposite Singapore.

A home in the residential district of Penang. The rustication on the facade recalls Renaissance architecture.

The Land "Down Under"

The first colonists of Australia were not always there voluntarily, and their memories of their homeland were still strong. This sentiment is emphatically conveyed by the houses that were built there from the 1830s on. The style of this architecture was first labeled Queen Anne, after the eighteenth-century monarch, and then Federation, in homage to the political system adopted in the far-off colony.

Whatever the name, the style is Victorian architecture. It is perhaps more modest in scale, often of only one story, but the handsome red-brick facades and roofs of gutter tiles framing dormer windows and tall chimneys remain. The plans are often asymmetrical, complicated by the insertion of turrets, verandahs, and balconies embellished with balustrades and wrought-iron decorations.

Climatic factors have resulted in a number of compositional variants and determined the choice of materials. In the subtropical climate of Queensland, greater use is made of wood, partly because of its availability and partly because of the difficulties involved in transporting brick and tile from the city. In some cases the roofs were made from painted corrugated iron, which makes air conditioning difficult. In New South Wales, on the contrary, slate, abundant in the area, is often used, together with stucco decorations inspired by eighteenth-century Italian architecture. Echoes of the Gothic and classical revivals that spread from Europe across the world in the nineteenth century are also evident.

These residences, functional but also representative in character, symbolize the possession of the territory. They are a mark of ownership, impressed by the colonists on the land. Today they bear witness to a vanished era. Many are open to visitors and, with the incomparable scenery that surrounds them, constitute oases of an older time.

Werribee Mansion in the vicinity of Melbourne, Victoria. The patio is built of large blocks of dark stone.

The main facade of Werribee Mansion. Set in the middle of a huge park, the residence was built in the second half of the nineteenth century by Thomas Chirnside, a prosperous sheep breeder from Scotland.

Government House, Sydney. The many-towered castle recalls the great structures of Scotland.

*Residence in Queensland.
The broad verandah
is lined by a long,
perforated screen that
transforms it into a
protected room.*

Entrance to a townhouse.

Convent House, Pokolbin. Built in the nineteenth century, it presides over a vast estate and is today used as a hotel.

Below:
Marnanie House, Melbourne.

Below center:
Como House, Melbourne.

Bottom:
Verandah of Withycombe House at Mount Wilson, near Sydney.

Overleaf:
Withycombe House, Mount Wilson. The extreme simplicity of its Victorian style is a fascinating contrast with the surrounding nature.

Above and right: Wood houses in Australia. The plentiful supply of wood made it an almost compulsory construction material.

Rippon Lea, Melbourne.
The building is a fine
example of twentieth-
century eclecticism.

Right:
Urban residence in
Melbourne. The
predominant building
pattern is characterized
by tall, narrow fronts
animated by loggias
and bow windows.

Far right: House at
Toowoomba, in the
hinterland of Brisbane.

Between London and Polynesia

New Zealand

Haere mai is the word for "welcome" in New Zealand, a land populated by Maori Polynesians twelve centuries ago, discovered by the Dutch explorer Abel Tasman in the seventeenth century, and explored again by the British navigator James Cook in the middle of the eighteenth century. A long way from the main trade routes, it was one of the last regions of the South Pacific to be colonized by Europeans. The first to arrive were seal hunters at the end of the eighteenth century, and afterward came the whalers. It was not until the first half of the nineteenth century that the *pakhena* appeared, European settlers who began to cultivate vast stretches of land.

In addition to their farming and organizational skills, colonists brought with them a taste for Victorian buildings. As was frequently the case, wood, available in large quantities, took the place of stone and brick. Often it was embellished with intricate carvings by the Maori; skilled in the plaiting of straw, the Maori provided the new arrivals with original designs and solutions for architecture and furnishing.

From Treaty House at Waitangi on North Island—perhaps the nation's first residence designed by an architect—to the early-twentieth-century Art Deco homes of Napier, the structures recall the long history and varied experiences of New Zealand. The houses that have been built over this time are often set amid meadows and woods; gardens have never been very popular, since the natural scenery consists of snow-clad peaks, glaciers, geysers, and volcanoes. The varied and luxuriant nature provides a wonderful setting for these elements of the British Isles transposed to this remote region of the Pacific, which, though on the other side of the world, has a misty climate that closely resembles the colonists' homeland.

New Zealand interior. The country has the same climate as Great Britain and so it was not necessary to adapt the architecture, although the residences are more colorful and allow themselves more stylistic liberties.

House in Auckland. The facade is lightened by a spacious loggia surmounted by paired windows.

Right, below center, and bottom: Three residences near Auckland. The gardens serve as a link between the house and the surroundings, as they do in the British Isles.

Building constructed from iron, wood, and brick at Rotorua, North Island.

Colonial structure in Rotorua.

*Overleaf:
The main facade of the Victorian Mangapapa Lodge, at Napier on the North Island.*

The drawing room of Mangapapa Lodge. It is located in a region with many vineyards.

The master bedroom of Mangapapa Lodge, which has been converted into a hotel. All of the furniture is original.

A simple construction in Rotorua.

The dignified and imposing doorway of a house in Rotorua.

Classical and austere residence in New Zealand.

New Zealand house characterized by informality and practicality.

Contemporary dwelling in Auckland. Some of its forms echo early colonial architecture.

The elegant main front of Alberton Mansion. The broad flight of steps leads down to a lawn ringed by tall trees located in the middle of a Romantic park.

PALLADIANISM AND NEOCLASSICISM

In the first half of the seventeenth century the English architect Inigo Jones launched a revival of the style developed by Andrea Palladio, based chiefly on a reinterpretation of his designs and writings. Although the work of the architect from Vicenza comprised public and religious buildings, it was his villas that most attracted Jones and prompted him to introduce the style into Great Britain. The Palladian style proved so popular that the elegant pronaoi and dignified colonnades of the late Renaissance soon made their way across the ocean to the North American colonies.

In eighteenth-century France, however, two currents of thought emerged and gradually spread throughout Europe. One, exalting spontaneity and instinct, was based on the thought of Rousseau and provided some of the cultural inspiration for the Romantic garden. The other was the rationalism of the Enlightenment, in which reason was seen as the highest essence of the spirit. In architecture, rationalism translated into a recourse to pure geometry. Cubes, spheres, and prisms became the elements of composition; the aesthetic perfection of Greek and Roman classical architecture was taken as a model. From this trend arose a new classicism that produced massive, severe buildings in which volumes were more important than ornamentation. Yet this neo-classical architecture was not a reinterpretation of classical antiquity such as had occurred in the Renaissance. Rather it was a slavish and pedestrian imitation that did no more than adapt the forms of the past to the needs of the present.

In the nineteenth century, when neo-Palladianism and neoclassicism spread to the British colonies, especially those in North America, the "noble simplicity and calm grandeur" of classical architecture was used for the facades of the settlers' new dwellings. At the same time ornamentation was reintroduced, producing effects that ranged from the picturesque to the decidedly eclectic.

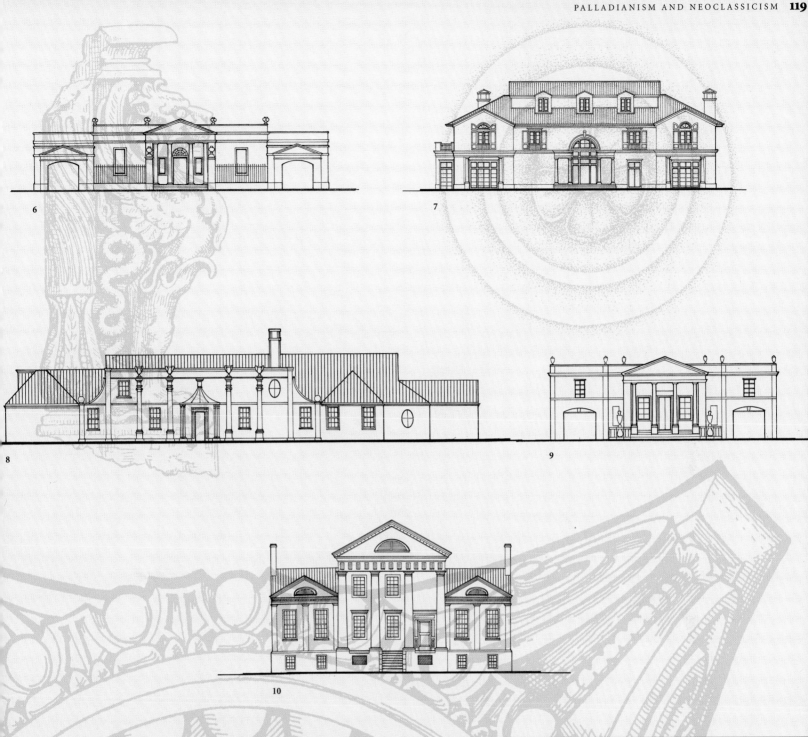

6

7

8

9

10

1. Monticello, Virginia.
Thomas Jefferson's home
is one of the most famous
neoclassical mansions in
America.

2. Neoclassical facade.
The style was widespread
in Massachusetts, and
the gigantic order proved
popular.

3. Greenberg Hall,
Connecticut, built in
1880 and 1881. The two
wings are linked to the
main block by a portico.

4. Urban residence in
Palm Beach, Florida.

5. Mansion in Newport,
Rhode Island, framed by
a tall colonnade.

6. House in Palm Beach,
Florida.

7. Mansion in Texas. The
wings are emphasized by
tympana.

8. House in Connecticut,
with side additions to the
center block.

9. Neoclassical residence
in Florida, featuring
columns, tympana, and
vases.

10. Turner Sounders
House in Town Creek,
Alabama, built between
1830 and 1835.

Spain's colonial enterprise began with the discovery of America. In 1493, just a year after Columbus's three caravels had landed on the island of Hispaniola, now divided between the Dominican Republic and Haiti, a colony was established there. This was followed by the conquest of Mexico, Central America, and Peru. Above all the Spanish were looking for gold and silver, minerals of great value and easy to transport.

In 1516 the future Emperor Charles V of Hapsburg ascended the Spanish throne. Under him and his son Spain reached the peak of its power and retained supremacy until the end of the century, when the country began to slip into decline, culminating in the invasion by Napoleon and the loss of all its colonies.

By the middle of the sixteenth century the gold rush had abated and the settlers began to consider the great potential of agriculture. It was in this period that the first buildings were constructed in the highly ornamented and stately style of the Spanish colonial baroque. Stuccoes, volutes, statues, and colonnades sprang up in places that had been devastated by the armies of Cortés.

From San Diego to the Last "Key"

New Spain

The viceroyalty of New Spain included all the territories north of the isthmus of Panama that were under Spanish control, covering a swathe of the modern United States stretching from San Diego to Florida. The latter is the most famous and exclusive vacation area in America and has survived a tumultuous history. Financiers, politicians, and artists continue their love affair with the state. Few cities in the United States possess images of splendor and opulence to rival those of Miami, Palm Beach, or Key West. Florida, chosen as an elite refuge by the American aristocracy in the early decades of the twentieth century, soon became an extension of Newport and a replica of Long Island.

In Florida, as in California, Arizona, and New Mexico, the mansions of the *conquistadores* who had founded New Spain were quickly joined by newer estates in the Hispanic style, which continued to celebrate the myth of a land bound to Spain and the Caribbean by ties of history and to the United States by those of politics. While Santa Fe and Taos are characterized by adobe architecture, the landscape of Florida from Miami down is all keys. One in particular has always attracted droves of visitors: Key West, the westernmost of the islands. On clear days it is almost possible to see the ninety miles to Cuba. Key West is the southernmost point of the United States and unquestionably the most Caribbean and Hispanic.

There are no great mansions on Key West, no opulence. The tone is subdued but elegant nevertheless. Ephemeral materials predominate, especially wood in the broad and airy patios, which take up entire house fronts and establish a dialogue between interior and exterior. The colors are equally notable: pale, pastel shades or beige and pink alternate with the blue tints of the sea.

Preceding pages:
The private courtyard of the Chichinequilla hacienda *at Querétaro, Mexico.*

Below:
Interior of the Martinez hacienda *at Taos, New Mexico. The adobe building dates from the eighteenth century and represents an interesting marriage of Spanish and indigenous architecture.*

The entrance to a mansion in Miami Beach. Concealed in a garden of palm trees, the house combines motifs typical of Spanish and Moorish architecture.

Above and left: Dwellings in Palm Beach, Florida. Decidedly eclectic, the local style is dominated by Spanish influences, especially in the decoration, freely interpreted with citations from a whole range of other styles and periods.

Villa Flora, on the seafront at Palm Beach. Although the windows are reminiscent of Venetian palaces, the architecture is derived from the Hispanic tradition.

A house built just outside Palm Beach at the beginning of the twentieth century. The double flight of steps leads to the main floor.

Overleaf:
The garden front of Casa Nana, Palm Beach, built between 1924 and 1926 by the architect Addison Mizner. Mizner traveled to Europe every year in search of new ideas.

Seaside facade of Mar-a-Lago.

Nuestro Paraíso, "Our Paradise," a home in Palm Beach.

The main entrance to Mar-a-Lago, in Palm Beach.

*Below and bottom:
Pediments in Taos, New
Mexico. Mediterranean
stylistic elements are
reinterpreted in adobe,
a material that permits
various styles of
decoration.*

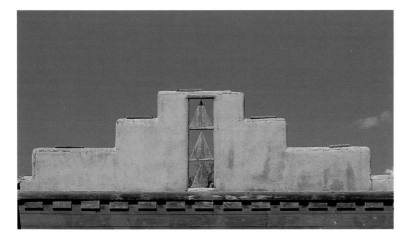

*An adobe house at Taos.
For centuries adobe
construction has
represented a successful
union of the Old and
New Worlds, offering free
rein to creativity and
yet still supporting
architectural traditions.*

Contemporary residence in Santa Fe, New Mexico. Adobe is still widely used for decorative touches on buildings in the region.

An unusual star-shaped window in adobe.

A "capital" in a historic building at Santa Fe. The structure is reminiscent of the models imported by colonists, but the decoration is entirely indigenous.

A thick wall around a house in Albuquerque, New Mexico. A few simple flowerbeds fill the space between the wall and the dwelling.

A townhouse in Santa Fe. A short flight of steps is the only decorative feature on the simple facade; the sculptural quality and the color of adobe are equally effective.

Pancho Villa's *Haciendas*

Below:
A corner of the garden
of Casa de la Torre, a
green oasis at the heart
of Cuernavaca, Mexico.

Bottom:
The kitchen of the
Oacalco hacienda *at*
Yautepec, one of the
oldest in the state of
Morelos, central Mexico.

Of all the houses in Latin America, the *haciendas* are the most suggestive and rich in history. The architecture is characterized by strong colors, squared forms, and spacious courtyards. Imposing groups of buildings, distinguished by marks of nobility, are scattered along the agave-lined roads of the country. Such structures are great farmhouses that preside over ranches that—before Pancho Villa and Emiliano Zapata's revolution in 1910—could reach the size of Belgium. People lived their wholes lives within the self-sufficient communities; the landowners were the leaders. Often, for miles around lay nothing but fields and pastures.

During the colonial period the size of these *haciendas*, of which the earliest examples date back to the seventeenth century, grew enormous. The complex would comprise, in addition to the master's house, the guest quarters, store, chapel, school, servants' quarters, granary, and blacksmith's shop, all laid out around the *corral,* or large courtyard. The largest *haciendas* had two of these courtyards: one for the servants and one for the owner. The *casco,* or *morada del patron,* literally the "master's abode," faced the *corral.*

The windows, often round or oval, were framed by bands of color or moldings of local dark stone. The walls were painted in bright colors or whitewashed in dazzling lime. Great importance was given to the stables, used to house the splendid horses that were the pride of the *hacendados.* The kitchens were large, and water, when the wells in the courtyards proved insufficient, was supplied by private aqueducts.

Today many of these *haciendas* still belong to the descendants of their founders. Some have been turned into hotels or convention centers, but many still serve their original purpose. They offer a journey into the history of Central America, as well as into a rural world that is fascinating in its isolation.

A solitary bench in
the casco *of the*
Chichimequillas
hacienda. The estate,
formed from a former
monastery at the end of
the eighteenth century,
is located near
Querétaro, Mexico.

Juriquilla, in the municipality of Santa Rosa at Querétaro, Mexico, one of nine haciendas *in the area. The owner's house and annexes are laid out around a large courtyard that has been turned into a garden.*

La Laja, another hacienda *at Querétaro. This thriving region in central Mexico has a large concentration of estates dating back to the Spanish period. This one is notable for its Pompeian red walls.*

The Juriquilla hacienda at Querétaro. Though the residence was recently converted into a hotel, its oldest structures—the long arcade and the baroque chapel—are almost intact.

Far left and left: The Chautela hacienda at Puebla, one of the best known. The residence is at the center of a vast property with many courtyards and porticos. The main facade is dominated by unusual neo-Gothic towers.

Antigua, the capital of colonial Guatemala. The city has more Spanish baroque buildings than almost any other in Latin America. The grandest are laid out around internal patios bristling with fluted pillars, friezes, and gleaming white stucco.

Street-side loggia in Antigua. Most such loggias faced the internal courtyards.

A courtyard in Antigua. The portico that surrounded it was partially destroyed by an earthquake in the 1980s. The monumental well at its center, reminiscent of the Renaissance cloisters of Europe, still stands.

Plantations and Adventurers

Greater Antilles

Above:
Stately house in Havana. During the period of Spanish rule, Havana was already the capital of a wealthy island that produced large quantities of sugarcane. Its large and elegant dwellings with ample porticoed courtyards offered an indispensable refuge from the summer heat.

Some of the most frequented islands in the Caribbean, Cuba, Santo Domingo, and Puerto Rico conserve precious relics of their colonial past. The cultivation and processing of tobacco and sugarcane, the slave trade, and later, North American tourism have made these places—both exceptionally beautiful and strategically located—a crossroads of history and culture. Verandahs, patios, charming little houses, and powerful fortified palaces are just a few examples of the traces that the colonists have left on these lands.

It is rare to find such a concentration of dwellings as the ones that face onto Avenida Quinta in Havana. In the last few miles before it reaches the old city, it is lined with a rich selection of elegant residences in the most disparate architectural styles. Built between the end of the eighteenth century and the early years of the twentieth, the houses range from Spanish colonial baroque and neoclassicism, which characterized the whole of the nineteenth century, to Art Nouveau and Art Deco, typical of the first decades of the twentieth. The ensemble is eclectic yet united.

Balconies, verandahs, and jalousies alternate with colonnades of local limestone or, more rarely, of marble or travertine imported from Europe. Graceful wrought-iron gratings cover the openings on the ground floor, which face onto simple gardens that are intended to frame the architecture rather than to be a mark of superiority over the equally elegant residences that line the Malecón, the famous boulevard that runs along Havana's seafront. Patios and porticos, natural defenses against the pitiless sun of the tropics, are prevalent.

Urban homes on Puerto Rico are quite different. While verandahs are also common on the streets of San Juan, gaily colored stuccos turn the city's elegant streets into drawing rooms, stages where people spend much of their day. Inside the oldest houses are courtyards with a well or fountain, the fulcrum of family life and a reminder of the fact that water in these islands is not just the source of life but a precious resource.

Entrance porch of a home in the residential quarter of Havana. Coats of arms, vases, and columns comprise the decorative repertoire of these mansions.

Casa San José in San Juan, Puerto Rico. Long uninhabited, it was restored at the beginning of the 1990s and turned into a hotel. The building stands in the historic center of the city and is laid out around a central patio with a fountain.

Staircase in Casa San José. Running alongside a small courtyard, the stair opens to a number of rooms, including what is now the dining room. The decor is very simple, with moldings in wood or stucco, wrought iron, and many bright colors.

A colonial residence on Avenida Quinta, Havana. The styles of the houses along the avenue are varied and often eclectic. One recurrent motif is the patio, usually bounded by columns and arches.

A neoclassical mansion in Havana. Brick and plaster simulate more costly stone, a material rare in Cuba and found only in the oldest buildings.

Interior of Casa Amparo
in San Juan, Puerto Rico.
The open beams and
vaulted doorways are
original.

Casa Amparo, now the
studio of a famous
ceramicist. The large
residence is located in
the city center. Its simple
street front belies the
succession of rooms
beyond, which stretch
to a far courtyard.

Overleaf:
An archway leading to
the terrace of the fort
of San Juan in Puerto
Rico, a large defensive
complex that once
included the residence
of the commandant.

An elegant residence in the heart of Havana characterized by arches, moldings, coats of arms, and stucco.

Casa Rosa in San Juan, Puerto Rico. The colonial residence has only recently been restored to its original splendor.

Balcony on a Puerto Rican townhouse. Hispanic in origin, such balconies (found facing private courtyards as well) are usually built of wood and roofed with the same materials as the rest of the house.

Baroque Viceroyalties

South America

Below:
Multi-hued window in Maracaibo. The bold range of colors in the city gives it a Caribbean air.

Bottom:
Colorful roof decoration, typical of Maracaibo. The architecture of the houses in the historic center is European.

From Maracaibo to Quito and from Lima to Buenos Aires are *haciendas* and *estancias* surrounded by oil fields, grasslands, and beaches of the finest sand. Some are still inhabited by their owners, and others have been converted into hotels or museums, but all of these elegant residences bear witness to the glories of the past in South America, a continent whose fortunes have always been linked to the land. In the "middle of the world," at an altitude of six thousand feet, the *haciendas* of Ecuador still belong to the historic great families of the Hispanic oligarchy. The rarefied fin de siècle atmosphere belies the fact that these residencies lie on the equator. In Argentina, the *estancias,* legendary ranches on the pampas, are ringed by endless expanses of fields and pastures.

It is perhaps in the colonial *barrios* of Maracaibo, among the brightly colored homes of the commercial middle class, that the South American spirit is expressed most forcefully and imaginatively. The architecture of this city represents a link between Europe and the Antilles, but it features a riot of colors that reflects the Venezuelan lifestyle of the past and present.

Thanks to Maracaibo's strategic position on the Caribbean Sea, the importance of its port has grown in proportion to that of the traders who flocked there. The city's wealth was created by merchants, shipowners, and adventurers. Their activities fostered the development of a bourgeoisie that saw the construction of elegant townhouses as a mark of distinction. While the building types and decorative motifs were imported from Europe, the colors were the strong and intense ones of the Caribbean and were often used in bold combinations. The new forms and colors of the residences, often ostentatious, were how the *maracuchos,* as the inhabitants of Maracaibo are called, cemented the union between their variegated new home and the far-off motherland.

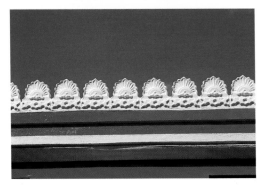

The Magdalena hacienda *in Ecuador. The isolated residence, located at an altitude of six thousand feet at the heart of a vast estate, is set against a backdrop of the Andes.*

The Immaculata Conception hacienda, Mérida. Located in a coffee-growing region in Venezuela, the main house is laid out around a furnished patio.

The Herreria hacienda, near Quito, Ecuador. The Spanish word herreria means brewery, and beer was indeed produced on the estate. Much of its furniture dates from the Spanish period.

The kitchen of the Quinta de Anauco, on the outskirts of Caracas. Its owners possessed a huge cocoa plantation nearby.

The verandah of La
Avelina, an hour's drive
from Quito. The
residence has recently
been opened to paying
guests.

Overleaf:
The Santa Filomena
hacienda *at Mérida,*
Venezuela. The large
courtyard onto which
the main house faces is
used to dry coffee beans
after the harvest.

The private chapel of the
Tandil hacienda at
Acelain in Argentina.
The large estate, nearly
7,500 acres of land,
comprises a village and
the large owner's house.

La Compañia hacienda
in Ecuador. The white
facade is convex and
features a pronaos. The
stairs lead into a large
garden.

The courtyard of an elegant residence in Cuzco, in the Peruvian Andes. Its powerful appearance is reinforced by the dark stone construction.

La Magdalena hacienda *in Ecuador. The white columns of the portico, which opens onto an inner courtyard, stand in contrast to the fired brick of the paving and roof tiles.*

El Recreo, at Valencia, Venezuela. The old colonial hacienda *has been restored and opened to the public.*

Above:
A porticoed courtyard at Trujillo, Peru. A single tree stands at the center, forming the centerpiece of the composition.

Opposite top: La Favorita estancia at Loma Verde, in the Argentinean pampas. Although built in the twentieth century, its forms recall the compositional and decorative motifs of the Spanish baroque.

Opposite bottom: Estancia in Argentina. Tall and slender columns characterize the facade, which is flanked by two later wings.

Far left:
The long arcade of the Herreria hacienda in Ecuador. The terrace faces a spacious garden.

Left:
A courtyard at Mérida, in the Venezuelan Andes. Each stately home had at least one courtyard; often a second was used by the servants.

A doorway with a broken tympanum in Trujillo, Peru. While it dates from the late eighteenth century, it is richly decorated and takes its inspiration from the Spanish colonial baroque.

A house facing the main square of Trujillo. The decoration consists of recessed windows framed by stucco moldings.

A doorway in Coro, a colonial city on the coast of Venezuela. The tapered columns and the tympanum, both triangular and curvilinear, are free interpretations of the classical tradition.

Classicism in Bamboo

The architecture of the Philippines is even more disparate than elsewhere in the former Spanish empire. Western styles and local traditions are blended according to personal tastes, producing suggestive dwellings that often feature an echo of Hispanic baroque and neoclassicism.

The myriad of small and large islands scattered over the immensity of the ocean, dominated by the main one of Luzon, makes the Philippines the most divided and at the same time the least Eastern country in Asia. Predominantly Catholic, it is full of examples of European architecture, sometimes happily married with the local style to produce a curious yet charming hybrid.

The townhouses of Intramuros—the original walled city of Manila, founded by the Spanish in the sixteenth century—have been inhabited by nobles and churchmen, adventurers and sultans, merchants and spies. Their residences have refined street fronts, but it is the internal patios that represent the best architecture of the time. The courtyard was the heart of the house and provided security and elegance, privacy and peace. Stone was widely used; it was often accompanied by wood, which the Filipinos have always worked skillfully.

Virata House in Manila is one of the more refined references to European architecture; built entirely out of gray stone, it has a broad pediment that runs along the whole of the facade. But the Philippines are a land of contrasts, sometimes of excesses, such as the legendary Malacañang Palace, former residence of Ferdinand Marcos. The Spanish and American colonists have left a profound mark on the architecture of this rich and charming land, but the traditional building material of bamboo has never been abandoned and, now back in vogue, characterizes the new Philippine style.

Top:
Interior of Virata House,
a stately residence in
Manila.

Left:
Roxas House in Manila.
The contemporary house
was inspired by the
European mansions of
the nineteenth century.

The balcony of a house
in Intramuros, the
colonial quarter of
Manila as well as its
original fortified nucleus.
The old Spanish houses
(some built as long ago
as the end of the
sixteenth century) make
extensive use of wood.

*The neoclassical main
facade of Virata House.*

*A pediment on the
facade of the
Malacañang Palace,
once the home of the
Marcos family in the
Philippine capital. It
was built by a Spanish
nobleman and in the
mid-nineteenth century
became the summer
residence of the Spanish
governor.*

The imposing and stately entrance hall of the Manila Hotel. The building is the enlargement of a colonial mansion, and some decorative elements from the original structure have survived.

1

2

3

4

5

6

7

8

BAROQUE VOLUPTUOUSNESS AND "TROPICAL MINIMALISM"

As its name suggests, the baroque is a "misshapen pearl," high-flown and often overblown. Yet it is a creative style, full of inventiveness. It was born out of a great need for faith, nurtured by the Reformation and Counter-Reformation, as well as an irrepressible joie de vivre. The baroque is a blend of sensuality and spirituality. The formal repertoire of this style is still that of the Renaissance, but it is handled in a new way. The surfaces are no longer composed according to classical rules but are brought to life with a new plasticity. Curved lines are widely used in the ani-

mated forms. Solids and voids alternate; corbels, columns, cornices, and string courses stick out or are recessed; concave shapes are placed alongside convex ones, creating indentations and projections. Space becomes dynamic, and decorations are used in abundance.

Inside the structures, the cunning use of light creates chiaroscuro effects and illusory perspectives, often enhanced by paintings and sculptures. The influence of the plateresque, the hyper-decorative style developed in Spain in the sixteenth century, is evident: wood, iron, and stone are skillfully "chiseled," producing a remarkable richness of detail. The late baroque and rococo styles would take this excessive decoration even further.

In the Spanish colonies in America, the indigenous artistic tradition revitalized the European baroque. New decorative elements were added to the canonical ones, and new forms enriched the already varied repertoire. The compositions became even more diverse and lavish.

In some cases, this profusion came to an end in the nineteenth century and the beginning of the twentieth. A sort of tropical minimalism emerged—before the word had been invented—and, drawing its inspiration from simple and elementary forms, reduced everything to the essentials. Cubes and parallelepipeds, for example, took the place of vibrant baroque walls. This more humble style was used chiefly in Colombian and Bolivian farmhouses.

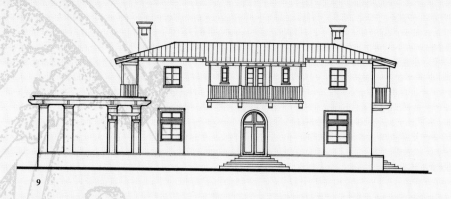

9

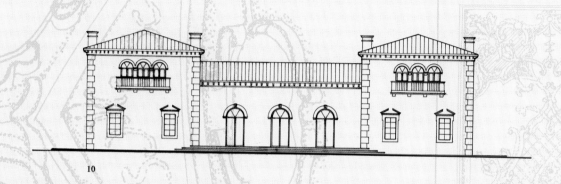

10

11

12

1. Vacation home in Miami Beach, Florida.

2. Single-story, street-facing residence in the center of Ponce, Puerto Rico.

3. Two-story house in Palm Beach, Florida.

4. Small vacation home on the Atlantic coast of Florida, both traditional and innovative.

5. The facade of the main house of the Garcíabajo hacienda at Caloto, Colombia.

6. Street facade in Ponce, Puerto Rico.

7. Neoclassical townhouse on Puerto Rico.

8. House in Palm Beach, Florida. The composition recalls the Hispanic neo-Gothic of the early twentieth century.

9. Porticoes and balconies on a residence in Palm Beach.

10. Vacation home in Florida. The wings feature triple-arched windows.

11. Spanish-colonial-inspired house in the Napa Valley in California.

12. Neoclassical stone portal around the entrance to a residence in the south of the United States.

France did not start to acquire colonies until the beginning of the eighteenth century. Most of the new territories then occupied by Europeans were in America; thus the French sent soldiers, hunters, and on occasion, missionaries to Quebec. Afterward the French occupied Louisiana and the western part of Hispaniola—St. Domingue (modern-day Haiti)—as well as Guadeloupe and Martinique in the Antilles.

In the early years of colonization, very few French people moved overseas, and they were scattered over vast tracts of territory, including Morocco and Algeria in North Africa. A foreign presence was institutionalized only in the nineteenth century; in fact, first the Revolution, then the Jacobin government, and finally the fall of Napoleon all dampened interest in the colonies.

In 1830, however, France began its conquest of Algeria and, between 1871 and 1914, extended its colonial empire to embrace around four million square miles and forty-seven million inhabitants in Africa, Indochina, and a few islands in the Pacific. The situation had changed a great deal since the time of the small Compagnie de Chine, founded in the seventeenth century; faced with the growing globalization of the economy, France was determined to play an important role.

Home of the "Backwoodsmen"

In the remote and unspoiled land of the Quebec region, spires, turrets, roof terraces, and pronaoi bristle from elegant mansions. The natural surroundings provide a frame for the houses, creating suggestive contrasts of color that are typical of Canada.

With the development of the trade in beaver skins, much in demand in seventeenth-century Europe—they were used to make warm and tough headgear—the indigenous inhabitants and the colonists of Quebec entered a long period of prosperity that contributed greatly to the expansion of settlement in the region. The backwoodsmen, or *coureurs de bois* as the French trappers who had initiated the colonization of Canada were known, adopted an increasingly sedentary way of life, finding it more convenient to purchase furs from the Native Americans; their compatriots were starting to cultivate land on the banks of the St. Lawrence River.

Most of the surviving architecture in Quebec dates from the nineteenth century. The dwellings look like little asymmetrical castles, vaguely Neo-Gothic in style, with towers and complicated pitched roofs. The materials include brick, stone (especially slate), and wood. The homes are surrounded by parks with thick woods and broad glades. Their owners came from the well-to-do families of Montreal, in whose hands much of the Canadian economy was concentrated. The stages on which they paraded their wealth were elegant townhouses in the center of the capital and pleasant country residences on the banks of the St. Lawrence or on Mont-Royal, the 763-foot "mountain" overlooking Montreal.

In the city of Quebec, also on the St. Lawrence, the largest houses were built on the Ile d'Orléans, directly opposite the city, which was famous even then for the relative mildness of its climate and fertility of its soil. Formal and typological references to Europe are immediately recognizable, yet the unusual use of materials and the distinctive combination of colors and decorative elements comprise a genuine *style québecois*.

Preceding pages: Terrace of Dar Moulay Boubker, a townhouse in Marrakesh owned by Xavier Guerrand-Hermès.

Below: Stone fountain in a Montreal garden.

Vacation home on Ile d'Orléans. Situated opposite the city of Quebec, the small island has always attracted its prosperous inhabitants.

Nineteenth-century residence set in a lush garden on Ile d'Orléans. Stone and brick alternate to produce a delicate two-color pattern.

Manor Howey, an elegant residence from the beginning of the twentieth century now converted into a hotel. It is built of wood and brick and has a spacious loggia opening onto the garden that separates it from the St. Lawrence River.

House on Ile d'Orléans. The simple but delicate decorations are in wood and stucco.

Corbels, towers, dormer windows, and chimneys typical of the homes of the commercial and farming bourgeoisie in Estrie. Wood, abundant in the area, is the principal construction material.

Vacation home on Ile d'Orléans. The exposed wooden structure is reminiscent of works of architecture in Brittany and Normandy.

House modeled on a French chateau. The mock rustication (the walls are actually built of plastered brick), tower, and painted roof help to give the dwelling its playful character.

House in Montreal. The entrance is marked by a structure with a tympanum, but the principal decorative motif is the rusticated ashlar of the facade.

Dwelling in a residential neighborhood of Montreal. Conical towers and exposed wooden beams make up the facade.

Opposite:
Vacation home set in its own park on Ile d'Orléans. Most houses on the island were built at the beginning of the twentieth century.

In the Deep South

The entrance to San Francisco Plantation, one of the most handsome of the houses located near the Mississippi River. Built largely of wood, it has a raised main floor reached by a double flight of steps.

The Great River Road passes through the plantations that line the banks of the Mississippi River, recalling the period of *Gone with the Wind.* The pre–Civil War era is reflected in the stately white facades, with their Ionic colonnades of the colossal order, pronaoi topped by triangular tympana, and quiet verandahs, where the silence is almost never broken.

Surrounded by white fields of cotton or brilliant green ones of slender sugarcane, these dwellings bring to life an important chapter in the history of the United States, a time when it was possible to accumulate immense fortunes and enormous estates. In the eighteenth and nineteenth centuries the planters of Louisiana were the richest in America and chose to build their homes in the classical Greek style, derived from British neo-Palladianism as well as from the architectural tradition inherited from the French, who had spent a long time in the region.

Residences like Nottoway or Madewood reveal their cultural debts in two-story open galleries, large mansards, dormer windows, and the broad pediments that always face the river, for many years the principal means of communication and plied by barges and steamboats even today. Oaks line the long avenues leading from the landing stage to the residence and sometimes surround the houses as well, creating a rarefied and highly suggestive atmosphere, especially in the fall when they produce the green cascades that have helped to make the area famous.

Another peculiarity of these plantations is the large amount of space set aside for guests. Distances were great and visitors would often spend the night. So the houses were equipped with a large number of bedrooms and other guest rooms, and sometimes spacious wings and annexes, that were furnished and decorated with the same care as the owner's accommodations. The Southern tradition of hospitality, based on comfortable appointments, personal attentions, and good cooking, has not vanished: it is still possible to experience it, especially by staying at one of the old colonial houses.

Rosedown Plantation. A long drive lined with oak trees ends at the formal garden, bounded by low hedges.

The drawing room at Nottoway, one of the finest residences in Louisiana. Even the floor and wooden columns are painted white.

The large kitchen of Hourmas House. Such facilities were usually located in small outbuildings adjacent to the main house, partly to avert the danger of fires.

A drawing room at San Francisco Plantation.

The dining room at Nottoway. During the period of French colonization, furniture was imported directly from France.

Wood fencing around the Nottoway Plantation. Such fences are a recurrent feature of the cotton plantations of Louisiana.

The facade of Madewood Plantation. Its dignified neoclassicism contrasts with the simple and informal wooden fence. Beyond the house, a low embankment holds back the waters of the Mississippi.

The verandah of the Destrehan Plantation. The building, completed in 1790, has massive foundations to help it withstand the frequent floods.

*Opposite top:
The river facade of
Nottoway Plantation,
White Castle. The double
verandah allows the
inhabitants to enjoy the
view of the Mississippi.
The dwelling was
completed in 1859 by
John Hampden
Randolph, a sugar
magnate.*

*Opposite bottom left:
Destrehan Plantation.
Located near New
Orleans, it has recently
been restored by the
River Road Historical
Society.*

*Opposite bottom right:
Ormond Plantation.
Standing in open
countryside, the house
is still in private hands.
It is characterized by
a double verandah
occupying the whole
of the main facade.*

*San Francisco Plantation, built on the
banks of the Mississippi
in 1856. Its Creole style
differs from the opulent
neoclassical dwellings
built in the prevailing
Greek revival style. A
small belvedere tower
is set in the middle of
the roof.*

*Longwood Plantation,
just across from
Louisiana in Natchez,
Mississippi. Its double
portico is supported by
slender coupled columns.*

Rosedown Plantation.
The long drive runs from
the public road through
the garden and up to the
house.

The vaguely Moorish
front of Longwood
Plantation.

Chretien Point, near Opelousas. Built at the end of the eighteenth century, it is surrounded by legends of hidden treasure and ghosts.

Bocage, a plantation on the route between Baton Rouge and New Orleans. Its layout is fairly simple, characterized chiefly by the spacious verandah on both floors.

Parlange Plantations, built by Marquis Vincent de Ternant in 1750 on a plot of land granted to him by the French crown.

Creole Comforts

The houses built by the French in the Caribbean are not just architecture; they represent a particular lifestyle. Verandahs, balconies, shutters, sunscreens, and overhanging eaves indicate that many daytime activities are performed in the open air, under a canopy providing refreshing shade from the sun or shelter from the downpours of the rainy season. The colors of the facades are the same as those of the surrounding nature: the blue of the sea and sky, the yellow and red of croton leaves, the pink of bougainvillaea flowers.

The construction materials also display great diversity: pink coral, pumice stone from the volcanoes, brick, teak, palm fronds for the roofs, and a great deal of corrugated iron. In some cases, the ground floor is built out of solid masonry, like the foundations, while the second floor is made of wood. The materials also indicate the internal functions of the house: fire-resistant stone and brick are used for the kitchens, while light and flexible timber minimizes the effects of the frequent earth tremors.

In the residences of Guadeloupe, Martinique, Haiti, St. Barthélemy, and the other islands ruled by the French, it is not possible to identify a truly Caribbean style. Rather there are many styles that vary according to the colonial influences and the local traditions. The varied styles emerged over the course of the seventeenth century and developed further during the following century, with the spread of colonial architecture. The most obvious features drawn from European precedents are the shutters, which took the place of the simple wooden panels used by the original inhabitants of the islands, and the symmetrical facades, which are laid out around the central entrance. In addition, the French introduced the dormer window, which added living space to the house and improved ventilation on the attic floor.

Ever since the time of Columbus, the Lesser Antilles, or West Indies, have been a constant surprise. They did not possess the riches that their discoverer had hoped for, but the natural environment—color, flavors, scents—has few equals.

Maison Clairière, at Fort-de-France, Martinique. The Creole home has a double verandah on the corner and a large mansard-cum-belvedere.

The dining room of the Clément habitation. The sugarcane plantation was built as early as the second half of the nineteenth century. The Clément family bought it at the turn of the twentieth century and built a rum distillery.

The interior of a house on Guadeloupe. The main structure is in wood with the exception of the foundations, built out of local stone. The furniture is partly imported and partly made on the island.

The hall of the Clément habitation, on Martinique, where the original owners still lived until recently. Many of the original furnishings have been preserved, and the house is now open to the public.

The living room of the Plein Soleil habitation, Martinique. It is now a hotel.

Leyritz Plantation on Martinique. The Leyritz family, originally from Austria, lived in Bordeaux before moving to the West Indies. The plantation first produced spices, then manioc, tobacco, and finally sugarcane. The residence has been converted into a hotel.

An annex of the Lagrange habitation, now a luxury hotel. The group of buildings is surrounded by a park filled with tall trees.

Below and bottom: Simple yet brightly colored decoration, typical of colonial houses on Guadeloupe.

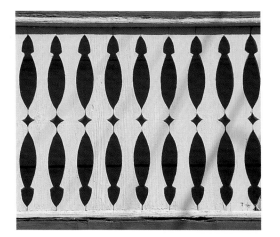

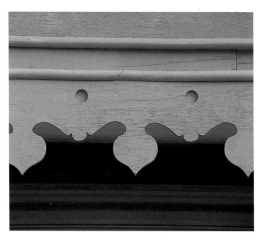

A wooden house on Guadeloupe. Set by itself on the top of a hill, it overlooks the sea on one side and an attached coffee plantation on the other. A small garden with a pool mediates between artifice and nature.

Far left:
Pool at Ceron Plan-
tation. The water is
used in the distillery
below. Ceron carries
out all phases in
the production cycle
of sugarcane.

Left:
The bell of the Clément
habitation on
Martinique, used to
announce mealtimes.

Maison Zevalos, built
entirely of iron and
brick. It was designed
by Gustave Eiffel for
a wealthy family
of sugarcane planters.

La Frégate, one of the
oldest houses at François,
on the southeast coast of
Martinique. Its existence
is recorded as early as
1704.

A small plantation
on Basse-Terre,
Guadeloupe.

The Beauséjour
habitation, *founded
in 1670.*

Overleaf:
A large plantation on
Basse-Terre, Guadeloupe.

A stately colonial facade on the island of Saint Martin, two-thirds of which remains French territory. The fretwork tympanum presents motifs typical of Creole architecture.

Opposite top:
The garden front of the Lagrange habitation. Built at the beginning of the twentieth century, its style is fairly unusual, with distinctive fretwork wooden turrets at each corner.

Opposite bottom:
An annex of the Plein Soleil habitation on Martinique. Located close to the sea, it is now a hotel.

The street front of a modest urban dwelling on Martinique. The colors of the Caribbean are always of great importance.

From Marrakesh to Tunis

Opening unexpectedly onto the narrow alleys of the Casbah are the doorways to residences of governors, viziers, courtiers, and wealthy merchants. The architecture of the *medina* (Arabic for "city") was inspired by the art of the Almohads, a Berber dynasty that ruled in northwestern Africa and Spain in the twelfth and thirteenth centuries.

Beautiful facings of glazed tiles and refined stuccoes (made from a mixture of plaster and lime) form elaborate decorations on walls and ceilings. Geometrical and plant motifs are often combined with mosaics and inscriptions from the Koran. The French colonists added little to this system of decoration.

A difficult relationship has always existed between northwestern Africans of Arab origin, who belong to independent tribes, and the Berbers. The unwillingness of the Arabs to accept central authority has created considerable tensions. Thus cities were ringed by tall, massive walls, and the houses built within them by the wealthy were also closed to the outside world. Few windows face the street; instead a large inner courtyard and a series of small light wells illuminate the residences, creating the impression of a city within the city. The extreme simplicity of the exterior contrasts with the complexity of the interiors, where rooms lavishly decorated with stuccoes, polychrome tiles, and *artesonados*—ceilings with carved, painted, and even gilded coffers—communicate through horseshoe, rounded, or pointed arches.

In these lands so rich in contrasts, including a climate where dry and hot winds off the desert alternate with cool and damp breezes blowing in from the Atlantic and Mediterranean, courtyards represent an oasis and a refuge. The interiors of the fragrant patios present an enchanted world, almost unimaginable in the context of the chaotic bustle of the Casbah. Inside the walls still exists a way of life that remains fabled in the West and that European settlers barely glimpsed.

Above left:
A window of Maison Majorelle, Marrakesh. The white-marble window is decorated with extremely fine carvings, and the same pattern extends to the grating.

Left:
The entrance to the garden of Maison Majorelle, now owned by Yves Saint-Laurent.

The main front of Maison Majorelle, built in the residential area of Marrakesh at the beginning of the twentieth century.

Maison Majorelle in Marrakesh. Modernist forms are fused with those of Islamic architecture, producing an unusual mixture of styles.

An asymmetrical fountain at the center of the patio of Villa Forbes, in Tangier.

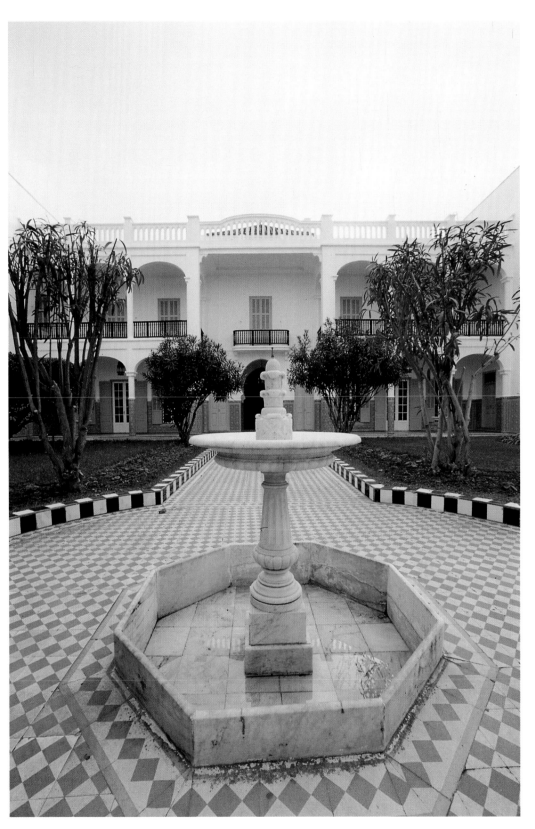

The swimming pool at Villa Forbes, in the splendid setting of the garden.

The Palais du Bardo in Algiers. The Arab dwelling was inhabited by the French during the occupation.

A delicately carved stone doorway leading to the private apartments in the Palais du Bardo. The door is thick and heavy to ensure privacy.

*Opposite left:
A colonial mansion built by the French in Algiers, now the seat of the French consulate.*

*Opposite right:
Mansions blending Arab and Western, especially French, styles. The large balcony is supported by finely decorated pointed arches.*

*Opposite:
Third-floor swimming
pool of the Dar Moulay
Boubker, in the medina
of Marrakesh.*

*A corner of the private
museum in the Hermès
townhouse in Marrakesh,
housing chiefly Arab
and Berber art.*

*A drawing room in the
Hermès townhouse,
now the home of Xavier
Guerrand-Hermès,
a keen collector of
period furniture. The
decorations are original
and date from the
nineteenth century.*

The upper part of a dresser in the Hermès house, Marrakesh. The piece is inlaid with semiprecious stones, rare woods, and mother-of-pearl.

Right:
Entrance to a hammam in the Dar Moulay Boubker, Marrakesh, framed by inlaid wood.

Far right:
Master bedroom in the Dar Moulay Boubker. Decorated with inlaid wood, the room features wall paintings and carpets.

The terrace of the Dar Moulay Boubker, which offers a view of Marrakesh.

Afrique Occidentale Française

Western Africa

Below:
A Moorish arch above a window in a colonial house at Dakar, Senegal. The detail shows the integration of Islamic architecture with the French style.

Bottom:
A wrought-iron "capital" supporting a verandah in Gambia.

The first contacts between Europe and western Africa took place in the first half of the fifteenth century, when Portuguese merchants explored the Cape Verde islands and the coasts of Senegal in search of wealth and trade opportunities. For a century and a half Portuguese ships were engaged in the profitable slave trade. In the seventeenth century the Dutch, English, and French arrived, establishing their dominance over the region. Throughout the eighteenth century thousands of natives were loaded on cramped schooners, specially converted for the purpose, and shipped to American markets, where they were put to work on the new coffee, cotton, and sugarcane plantations. The often corrupt local rulers ignored or even supported the traffic in humans. In fact slavery had long existed in Africa, but the Europeans organized it on a worldwide scale, making enormous profits.

In 1815 trafficking in slaves was abolished at the Congress of Vienna. The search for new sources of wealth in agriculture did not yield any appreciable results until Louis Faidherbe was appointed governor in 1845 and introduced the cultivation of peanuts. This was an immediate success, and within ten years the administration of the colony had attained autonomy. The new plantations brought with them a new set of elegant residences, which were built alongside those erected by the slave traders. When the French moved into the African interior in the second half of the nineteenth century, Senegal became the home base for their expeditions and a place of transit for merchandise.

Thus the colony of Afrique Occidentale Française, or French West Africa, was born. The cities took on a more monumental and decorous appearance. From Senegal to Mali and the Ivory Coast, the settlers' houses became more stately, acquiring loggias, balconies, and gratings to screen the sun and provide ventilation. The French colonial style was adopted by the indigenous people as well, who saw it as a mark of distinction. As in many European territories, the result is a fascinating blend of different and distant experiences.

A mansion on Gorée, the island off Dakar harbor where the colonists settled before conquering the mainland, also known as the "island of slaves."

House in Ziguinchor, a delightful colonial town on the Casamance River, in the south of Senegal. The architecture is a blend of the Portuguese and French colonial styles.

Annex of an upper-class residence in Ziguinchor. The mock rustication is emphasized by the bold two-color pattern of the walls.

A house on Gorée Island, off Dakar. The small patio is enclosed on three sides by the residence and on the fourth by a high wall with a door.

A dwelling on Gorée. From the outside, only a balcony reveals the presence of the garden.

House on Gorée Island. The first houses built on the island are notable for their massive, fortress-like walls, strong colors, and few openings, softened only by the color.

A Moorish arch framing a doorway in Dakar. The fine wrought-iron lacework supports a clock.

A clock set into a pediment, simply decorated with brick and plaster, in Dakar.

A Senegalese house standing before a high wall of rock. The main facade faces the sea.

A townhouse on Gorée Island. The long balcony faces the main square.

A small colonial house at Ziguinchor. During the colonial period, the Senegalese town was an active trading post.

Malagasy Pomp and French Grandeur

In 1513 the Portuguese navigator Pedro de Mascarenhas was the first European to visit the island of Réunion, lending his name to the archipelago. Over the following century the islands were visited by the Dutch, English, and French. The French decided to institutionalize their presence in the first half of the eighteenth century, founding an official colony. And so large coffee, vanilla, and sugarcane plantations were established on Réunion, as well as on nearby Mauritius.

The homes of the Malagasy queens contrast with the patios and verandahs of the colonial houses on the Mascarene Islands and with the residences that the French built on Réunion, in valleys and on plateaus that are now dotted with their unusual colors and forms. They are almost as varied as the indigenous peoples of Madagascar, of Indonesian, Indian, African, and French heritage. The facades are more austere; in the majority of cases the staircases are built of wood and located on the exterior, leading to balconies. To a contemporary eye, the palaces seem almost antiquated, reduced in scale, warped in proportion, and "poor" in materials.

The vacation homes of the Malagasy royalty and nobility can still be seen at Tamatave, an important port on the east coast and a center for French trade, where vanilla, sugar, timber, and semiprecious stones were shipped back to Europe. But in the town, now called Toamasina, the seaside residences left by the French after their expulsion in the 1970s are abandoned and decayed; the history of the island's colonization can be read in their simple and porous mortar.

A small house at Saint-Denis on the island of Réunion. Built at the beginning of the twentieth century, its entrance is set in a projecting section topped by a sort of turret.

A colonial mansion in the hills around Antananarivo, Madagascar.

The Mascarin complex
on Réunion, which is
surrounded by a
luxuriant garden. The
paving consists of
blocks of lava.

Below:
House in the center of
Saint-Denis.

Bottom:
The Maison Rouge, in
the south of the island of
Réunion.

One of the last French colonial houses on the seafront at Toamasina, on the Indian Ocean coast of Madagascar. Many such residences date from the period of the port's greatest prosperity, the decades between the two world wars.

The main facade of the Villa Mascarin, on Réunion. It is set in a lush garden.

An urban residence surrounded by a park in the center of Saint-Denis, on Réunion. Entrance to the house is through an arcade.

An elegant dwelling built with the island's typical red mortar at Antsirabe.

The Villebague sugar refinery, one of the first to be built on the island of Mauritius. The owner's house dates from the middle of the eighteenth century.

A sugarcane plantation in the center of the island of Réunion. The main house consists of a long low section linking two tower-like blocks at the sides.

The dining room of the Chateau de Labourdonnais, on Mauritius. The walls are painted with trompe l'oeil scenes of rural life.

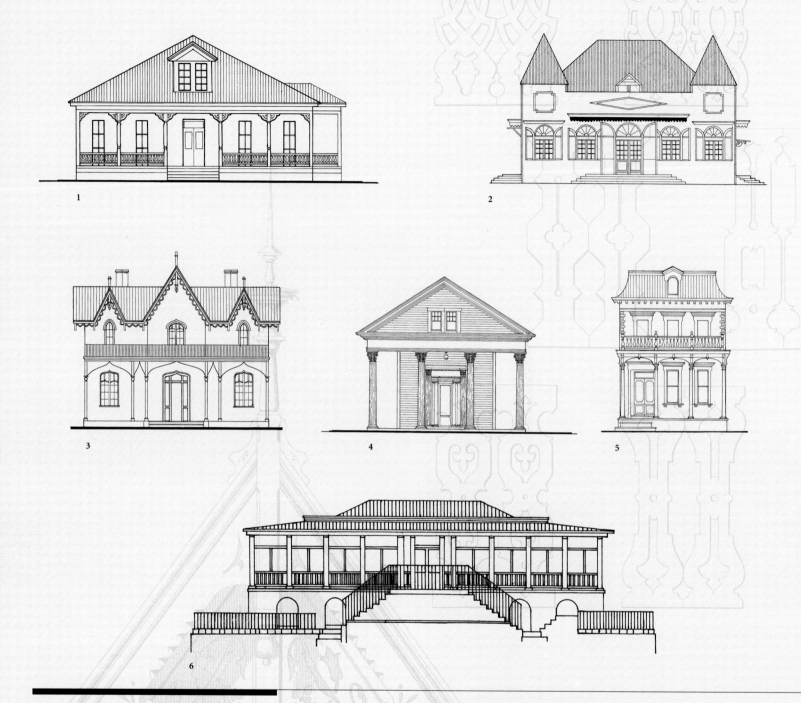

1

2

3

4

5

6

BEAMS AND LACE

The climatic conditions and plentiful supply of timber in many of the regions conquered by the French induced the colonists to construct chiefly in wood, instead of the brick, stone, and marble preferred in Europe. Even the building techniques were often modified to adapt to the different woods available locally. Two developments had an influence on the construction of wooden dwellings: the mechanization of sawmills and the invention of nail presses. The introduction of the steam-powered circular saw between the end of the eighteenth century and the

beginning of the nineteenth began the production of lightweight, jointed lengths of lumber for architectural use. The procedure adopted by the settlers was the same as the traditional European method, used since the end of the sixteenth century. It entailed making a supporting skeleton out of wooden crosspieces and uprights, which was assembled on the ground and then raised. Side beams supported the floors and roof frame. Joints were made by shaping the ends of the members so that they fitted into one another and ensured the rigidity of the structure. Nailed joints came into widespread use at the beginning of the nineteenth century. Thus wood was an ideal material for the construction of the colonists' houses. However, a house had to be not only solid

and functional but beautiful as well. So skilled craftsmen cut wood into intricate and lacy patterns to decorate the facades of the new residences. This fretwork was used to underline eaves, support verandahs, or create banisters and ventilation screens, and thus became a cheap but attractive form of decoration. When wood was in short supply, or it became more economical to use iron, the metal was forged or cast in molds and then plated with tin or lead to increase its resistance to corrosion. The material's low cost and ease of assembly led to its extensive use.

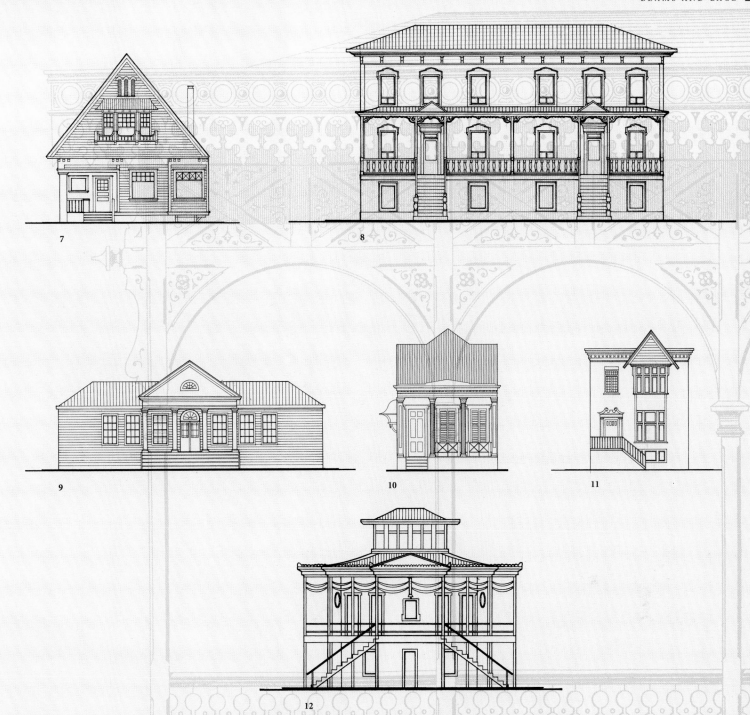

7

8

9

10

11

12

1. A small house with a porch and mansard in Quebec.

2. Villa Timol at Saint-Denis, a late-eighteenth-century dwelling.

3. Dr. Charles Bonner House at Holly Springs, Mississippi, built in 1857.

4. House in Louisiana. The tympanum is bigger than the house itself, which is the size of the naos of a Greek temple.

5. Townhouse in Los Angeles.

6. Maison Fournier on Guadeloupe. A double staircase leads to the main floor, and the spacious verandah opens onto the garden.

7. A small Californian house halfway between tradition and innovation.

8. A large house in Quebec.

9. A neoclassical residence built of wood on the Mississippi River.

10. A wooden Creole residence in New Orleans.

11. Small house in Quebec. Tall and narrow with an off-center entrance, this building nevertheless has a tympanum and cornice.

12. Steamboat House, erected in a French-Chinese style in New Orleans in 1857. In 1912 the son of the man who built it had an exact copy made, and the two buildings, still belonging to the same family, stand next to each other.

Portuguese Colonial Style

Along with the Spaniards, the Portuguese were the first Europeans to found colonies. Great navigators and explorers, they plowed half the world's seas in the fifteenth century, gathering a notable harvest of information for the cartographers of the time.

Like their Spanish neighbors, the Portuguese at first showed a preference for places where gold and silver could be found, and it was not until they had consolidated their presence that they began to cultivate the land, exploiting such profitable crops as coffee, cocoa, and rubber in America, and to develop trade in the Asian ports of Melaka and Macau.

The architecture adopted by the Portuguese in their colonies is less stately than that of the Spanish, and somewhat subdued in tone. The volumes are more contained and the forms less elaborate, and the decoration relies mostly on color, often in bright and strongly contrasting shades.

After the period of the great discoveries and the early colonies in the sixteenth century was over, Portugal entered a long period of decline. In 1578 the country was annexed by Spain, finally regaining its independence only to be occupied by Napoleon's troops. In the meantime, its overseas territories slowly vanished.

"Fazendas Cafeeiras"

After the exhaustion of the richest gold mines in the state of Minas Gerais, many entrepreneurs saw great possibilities for profit in coffee and rubber production, investing large sums in it. This led to the development of Manaus, the rubber capital in the heart of Amazonia, and the coffee-growing region to the south, in the state of Rio de Janeiro.

Production of the precious beans increased to such an extent that by 1870 Brazil held a world monopoly. Large *fazendas,* as the Portuguese called their plantations, were gradually established in the rolling hills around Rio, far from the plains. Starting with a simple colonial house prototype—which opened onto a verandah and was stoutly built, with a pitched roof, whitewashed walls, and brightly colored door and window frames—architects developed more complex and varied designs, using compositional elements drawn from the European architectural lexicon.

Though showing a certain predilection for eclectic forms, the dominant style is neoclassicism, adapted to suit the local materials and simplified, due to a shortage of skilled workers. Most building types are horizontal and emphasize the presence of the main floor. They are laid out symmetrically around the entrances, which are marked by flights of steps, porticoes, roof terraces, and columns. The decorative elements, used as a sign of refinement, include columns and pilaster strips, stringcourses, capitals, cornices, and moldings around doors and windows. All are very simple, since the absence of marble or other kinds of hard stone made it difficult to carve elaborate ornaments. The way they are combined, however, distorts their proportions and pattern and produces a composition that is sometimes fanciful and charming, and other times clumsy and incoherent. The more refined elements, such as statues, lampposts, wallpaper, marbles, and bathroom fittings, were imported directly from Europe, in particular from France and Italy. As in the legendary Opera House in Manaus—where Enrico Caruso and Sarah Bernhardt performed—the result was an eclectic and suggestive collage of pieces brought from the Old World, a style that was used in the empire of coffee to symbolize wealth and power.

Preceding pages: Portuguese houses on Taipa, an island off Macau.

Below: The Secrétario fazenda at Vassouras, in the state of Rio de Janeiro. The interiors were famous for luxurious furnishings.

The driveway leading to the São Luiz da Boa Sorte fazenda, at Vassouras. Horses are also bred on the large estate.

The São Policarpo fazenda at Rio das Flores, in the state of Rio de Janeiro. It has recently been restored after a long period of neglect.

The São Fernando fazenda at Vassouras. The large nineteenth-century complex and a number of outbuildings stand on an embankment.

The Paraíso fazenda.
On the exterior are
simple ornaments;
inside, the walls are
decorated with mock
marble painted on
plaster.

Overleaf:
The São Fernando
fazenda at Vassouras.

Elements of baroque architecture on a building at Itaguaí. The volutes, elaborately shaped windows, and stuccoes are derived from seventeenth-century European architecture.

A detail of the Itaguaí fazenda, *now used by the local university.*

View of the Vassouras
area from the São
Fernando fazenda. In
the past the hills were
covered with coffee
plantations, but today
the crops are diversified.

The Pau Grande fazenda
at Avelar, in the state of
Rio de Janeiro. The estate
was founded in 1709,
but it was not until the
end of the century that
the production of coffee
intensified.

An annex of the Secrétario fazenda *at Vassouras. The clock incorporated into the structure was imported from Paris.*

The private, garden facade of the Secrétario fazenda. *The paths through the garden are bordered by numerous colored flowers.*

The two-tone front of the *São Luiz da Boa Sorte* fazenda. *The custom of using blue to emphasize the decorative or functional elements on facades is common in the state of Rio de Janeiro.*

Santa Justa fazenda. *One of the plantations at Rio das Flores, it was long owned by the baronial family of the same name.*

The Santa Genoveva
fazenda *at Rio das*
Flores. Built at the end
of the nineteenth
century, it is flanked by
a small private chapel.

Timber Island

Madeira

The small archipelago was visited by sailors even in ancient times, but its systematic settlement did not begin until 1419, when the main island was given the name of *ilha de lo legname* ("timber island"), or Madeira. Funchal, the capital, was built about a century later. Apart from brief periods of rule by the Spanish and the British during the Napoleonic era, the island has belonged to Portugal ever since. Renowned for the year-round mildness of its climate, it has been not only a source of profit but also a charming vacation resort, and one located not all that far from Europe. Today it is an autonomous region of the Portuguese state.

Farmhouses and neoclassical residences, surrounded by lush tropical vegetation, dot the slopes of Madeira. But it is the *quintas,* the large country houses built by the Portuguese colonists to seal their ownership of the lands awarded to them, that dominate the island's architectural history. These manor houses closely resemble their equivalent in the Old World. They have large, screened windows, embellished by the subtle use of two colors, entrances marked by flights of steps and canopies over the doors, and string-courses, friezes, and cornices built out of lava.

In a land where the local climate varies greatly from place to place—from banana plantations to vineyards and sugarcane fields, from hydrangeas to jacaranda trees—nature has always played a decisive role in shaping both the landscape and the architecture. Thus, in the countryside, opulent official residences alternate with sober farmhouses enlivened by shady patios and enchanting romantic gardens. The famous *azulejos,* the blue-and-white glazed terra-cotta tiles found all over continental Portugal, have not proved so popular here, and they are more as a nod in the direction of the homeland than an important decorative feature.

Water flowing from a mask in the garden of the Quinta do Palheiro, in the vicinity of Funchal.

The chapel of the Quinta do Palheiro. The two-tone pattern created by two different kinds of stone extends to every building in the complex.

Villa Berardo on its hilltop site. A pathway paved with volcanic stone leads to the vaguely Victorian edifice.

One of the grottoes carved out of the rock wall next to Villa Berardo. Sponges and pebbles alternate with stuccoes and azulejos.

The terrace alongside Villa Berardo. The grottoes are on the left, and the garden covers the hillside on the right.

The main facade of the Quinta do Palheiro. Built in the nineteenth century, it lost its agricultural role long ago and today is a residence. The garden is open to visitors.

A residential courtyard
in the center of Funchal.
In the capital, many
nondescript buildings
conceal elegantly
decorated interiors or
plant-filled courtyards.

The garden front of the
Quinta Splendida,
enlivened by a delicate
two-tone pattern. The
house stands next to
a tourist resort.

The Quintas da Nazareth, which has recently been restored. Once located outside the built-up area of Funchal, it is now ringed by new construction.

Gateway to the East

Decoration on a house in Melaka. The prosperous Portuguese merchants of the sixteenth and seventeenth centuries demanded opulence from their designers.

Until the fifteenth century Melaka was a small and insignificant settlement of fishers. Around 1400 Prince Paramesvara, fleeing from his kingdom of Tumasik, took refuge there and turned it into an important port and active trading center, the most cosmopolitan not just on the Malay peninsula but in the whole of Southeast Asia. It was here that Arab and Indian traders came with fabrics, carpets, and jewelry, and those of the Indonesian archipelago with camphor, nutmeg, cloves, and sandalwood. The city had quarters for Arab, Chinese, Indonesian, and Thai merchants.

Such prosperity drew the Portuguese to Melaka, who conquered it in 1511. They maintained their domination of the city for over a century, until their place was taken by the Dutch and then by the British. The colonial powers were interested in Melaka largely due to its strategic position at the point where the northeast and southwest monsoon winds met; it was therefore a port of call on many different routes of navigation.

The city experienced its period of greatest wealth and splendor under the Portuguese. Trade flourished, the merchants made profits, and there was stable government. Part of the city's success was due to this stable government, which divided power between the white rajahs and the local chieftains. The integration of political and economic power led to a cultural interchange that brought about an interesting metamorphosis in architecture.

The size and number of openings were increased to improve ventilation, ceilings were raised to obtain the cooling effect produced by greater volume, and balconies were introduced. Large, and covered to provide shade, the balconies extended the length of the front facade, and sometimes surrounded the entire house. Marble was replaced by local stone and often by wood, which was plentiful in the region and widely used in indigenous architecture. The roofs sloped, as they did in Europe, where winters were cold and wet. In Melaka, the sloped roofs channel the abundant rainwater and also help to create an insulating chamber that serves as a defense against the sun. The sleepy atmosphere of contemporary Melaka is redolent with memories of the past; its houses are now used as vacation homes by the businesspeople of Kuala Lumpur.

Residence in Melaka with a two-tone pattern of white walls and decorative bands, a composition typical of Portuguese dwellings.

Freely interpreted mannerist and baroque elements on a residence in Melaka.

The Governor's Palace near the harbor. Splendidly restored, it is open to the public.

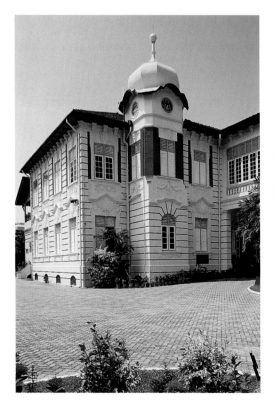

Decorative details on a Melaka residence. Often constructed from materials unfamiliar to their builders, such edifices have not always withstood the test of time.

*Far left:
A pronaos on stocky fluted columns, leading to an entrance.*

*Left:
The double portico of a house in the city center. Decoration is reduced to a few touches of color.*

Portugal in Asia

Macau

Macau was the first European colony to be established in Asia. Founded in 1557 by a few Portuguese traders who were on good terms with the Chinese emperor, it developed rapidly and soon became the main center for European trade with the Far East. In the sixteenth and seventeenth centuries Catholic missionaries arrived in the wake of the merchants and made it the base for their attempts to convert China and Japan to Christianity.

In the eighteenth century the Netherlands tried several times to wrest the lucrative monopoly from the Portuguese but did not succeed. At the same time, the colony became the summer residence of the "tai-pans," merchants based in Canton who rested in Macau between trading seasons, which were dependent on the winds. Macau's prosperity lasted until 1841, when the British founded Hong Kong with the avowed intent of challenging Portuguese hegemony. Following the Chinese revolution in the twentieth century, the colony took in many refugees, and during World War II, it became a refuge for Westerners fleeing the Japanese invasion of Hong Kong.

The evidence of the past is still plainly visible in Macau: the plaster on old colonial buildings, while flaking, is still brightly colored and immediately recognizable among the Chinese temples and skyscrapers. Ochers and bright yellows enliven the classical orders of townhouses and government buildings, testifying to the endless evolution of pure forms when married to local materials, climates, cultures, and tastes. Macau's gardens have been designed in the Chinese tradition to nourish the heart, calm the emotions, and still the mind. They echo nature in miniature, with rocks as mountains and pools as lakes.

Even after the first signs of decline were noted, Macau continued to grow, spreading onto the nearby islands. A series of elegant little houses was built on the tree-lined and stone-paved promenade of Taipa in the 1920s by wealthy members of the Chinese bourgeoisie, who sought refuge from the noise and bustle of the city. Steeped in an aura of charmed tranquillity, the residences on Taipa reflect the peace of mind of those who continue to invest in the former colony.

Wrought iron, stuccoes, and sinuous forms on the facade of a house in central Macau.

Luo Lim Ieoc, a large garden with a small attached house. Corinthian colonnades flank the circular doors, which prevent evil spirits from entering.

Bela Vista, Macau. The old house, facing the harbor, went through a long period of decline before being beautifully restored.

Vacation home on Taipa, an island dominated by second houses belonging to the wealthy citizens of Macau. The streets are still paved with stone, and all residences are painted in shades of green and white.

A terrace of the Bela Vista, now an elegant hotel. Some of the original furnishings were preserved to maintain the colonial atmosphere that has long characterized the interiors.

Palm trees outlined against a townhouse in the center of Macau. Buildings, pilasters, capitals, and arches are all finished in unprecedented colors.

European-style decoration on a Macau residence. Stucco and plaster do not stand up well to the incredible humidity of the Far East.

Right and far right: Brightly colored houses in Macau.

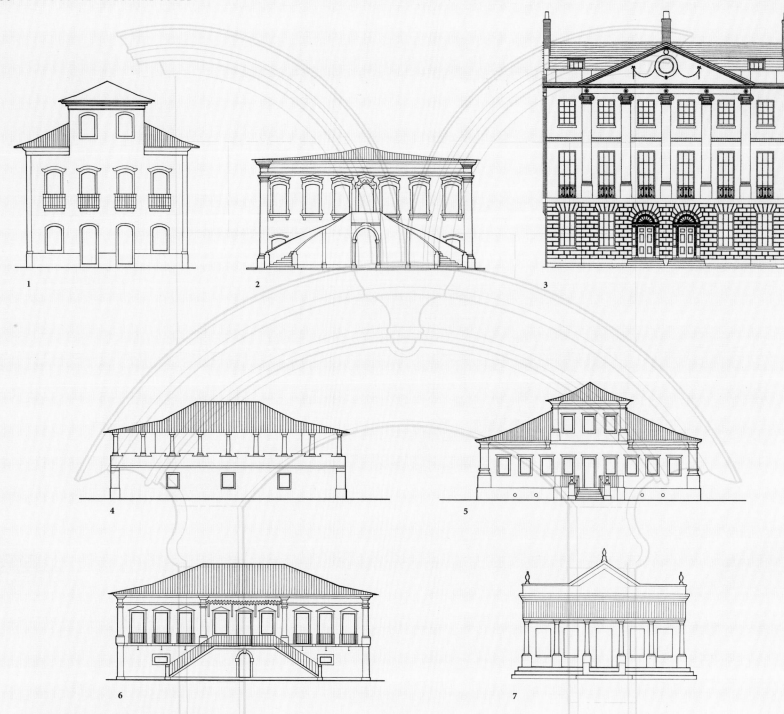

FOUR MODELS FOR A *FAZENDA*

Improvised tools, local building materials, and Portuguese and indigenous construction: traditions are the ingredients of Brazilian residential architecture. Military architects, sent from Lisbon to erect fortifications, also designed houses. Master builder Luís Diaz, one of these architects, perhaps made the greatest contribution.

The architects who came in the retinue of the royal family in 1808, on the other hand, brought with them neoclassical influences that were to characterize the whole of subsequent colonial architecture in

Brazil. The principles of the new style were taught at the Imperial Academy of Fine Arts, founded in 1826, and from there spread throughout the country.

It is possible to distinguish four models among the various *fazendas* built between the second half of the eighteenth century and the early part of the twentieth century. The first is derived directly from the sugarcane plantations of the eighteenth century. It has a central block to which verandahs and chapels are added haphazardly. The whole is an assemblage that has been built up over the course of time to meet practical rather than aesthetic needs. The second type has a compact structure surmounted by a high roof. The main facade features a verandah running its entire length; the residence stands on a basement that

raises it above the ground. In more elaborate examples, the verandah is supported by columns rather than pillars. The third model is typical of the large residence. Harmoniously proportioned, with a pleasant balance of solids and voids, it has a rational distribution of doors, windows, and balconies, which are often linked by decorative bands. Moldings emphasize the compositional elements. The fourth model—the most varied—has a single story with a large dormer in the middle, almost a second floor, which is used as living space. This type of building was much in vogue in mid-nineteenth-century Rio and gradually spread from there to outlying areas.

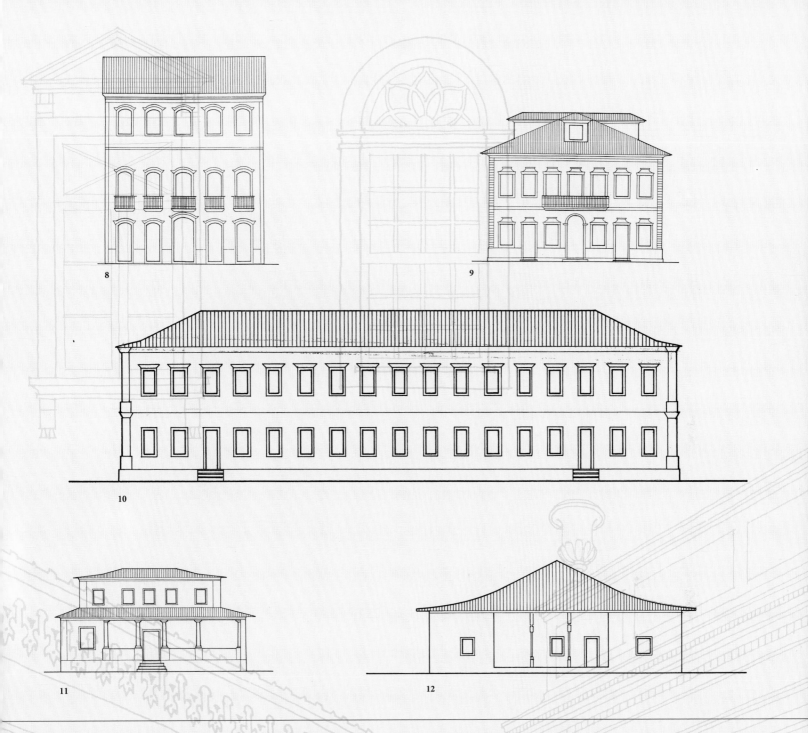

1. An urban residence in Brazil.

2. A suburban dwelling in the state of Rio de Janeiro.

3. A nineteenth-century townhouse in Rio de Janeiro.

4. The Pau D'Alho fazenda, *one of the first to cultivate coffee. A verandah runs around all sides of the building.*

5. *The facade of the São Laurenço* fazenda *in the state of Rio de Janeiro.*

6. A double staircase providing access to the Tres Rios fazenda.

7. Three vases atop a small colonial residence.

8. A nineteenth-century middle-class townhouse in Rio de Janeiro.

9. A suburban residence in Brazil.

10. An imposing neoclassical fazenda.

11. An asymmetrical portico on a small house.

12. A simple rural dwelling fusing both colonial and indigenous styles.

The first threat to Spanish and Portuguese colonial dominance came from the Dutch, who founded New Amsterdam. The British did not look kindly on the presence of the Dutch on the Atlantic seaboard. War broke out in 1633, and New Amsterdam passed into the hands of the duke of York, who gave it his name.

Unlike Spanish and British colonists, the Dutch preferred commerce to territorial and military conquest, and their first contacts with foreign lands often took place under the banner of trade. Instead of founding colonies they set up joint-stock companies—such as the East India Company—which were authorized by the crown first to conduct trade and then to settle, conquer, administer, and defend territory. The buildings constructed by the Dutch overseas are characterized chiefly by their pediments and gables, based on the style that developed over the same period in Amsterdam and Rotterdam. The settlers in South Africa were fairly faithful to their roots. In the Antilles, colonists used the old forms but were much more daring in their colors. In the Indonesian archipelago, the Dutch encountered a strong and highly developed architectural and artistic tradition, and the result was an intriguing compromise.

A Caribbean Amsterdam

In the seventeenth century officers of the Dutch navy, who had been instructed to colonize the best islands in the Caribbean, chose Curaçao as their headquarters. It was from this tiny island that the Dutch crown's interests in the Caribbean were administered, and it soon became one of the most prosperous islands in the archipelago. Later the Dutch acquired Bonaire and Aruba, principally to provide greater security for Curaçao and its capital, Willemstad.

The three islands did not possess great natural resources, but within a short space of time they achieved a dominant position in the region. The capital is still a seventeenth-century Amsterdam in miniature. Its tall, narrow baroque pediments, facades painted in lively colors, and purple pitched roofs give it a unique character. Its streets are so well maintained that they almost look like theatrical scenery.

The great wealth of the Dutch derived chiefly from the slave trade. The island was a distribution center where ships arrived from Africa and the merchants and colonists of the Caribbean went to purchase what they needed. The profits from the slave trade were reinvested in sugarcane plantations of vast sizes, which employed slaves as the cheapest form of labor.

Toward the end of the seventeenth century Curaçao was declared a free port, which brought about a rapid increase in the number of ships that visited the island—on occasion, the number would reach one hundred a day. Over the following centuries banking activities assumed ever greater importance, and so the island was enriched with more and more elaborate and interesting works of architecture. These were inspired by the Netherlands in their forms and the Caribbean in their colors, always strong and highly contrasted. The bright colors create on the streets of Willemstad the illusion of a shop window of an imaginative confectioner, in which a series of intricately decorated cakes are displayed.

Preceding pages: Boschendal farm at Franschhoek, near Cape Town.

Below: Brievengat landhuis (country house) on Curaçao. Long the residence of Dutch settlers, it has been turned into a restaurant and colonial museum.

The living room of Brievengat. The simplicity of the interiors is enlivened by the furnishings, some of which were imported from Europe.

A typically Dutch gable at the Ceritu farmhouse on Curaçao.

Papaja, a landhuis *converted into a restaurant. The Pompeian-red tone almost blends into the woods behind.*

Konigsplein on Curaçao. In the Dutch tradition, the house is set on an embankment; access is provided by a flight of steps that serves as the principal decoration.

The Savonet farm on Curaçao. One flight of steps rises from the countryside to the terrace on which the farm buildings are set; another leads to the main house.

Top:
The mailbox at
Brievengat.

Above:
Sloping dormer window
with a gable, on the
roof of Savonet landhuis
on Curaçao.

An urban dwelling in
Willemstad.

The pediment of *Chobolobo* landhuis *on Curaçao, now swallowed up by the suburbs of Willemstad. Terminating in conspicuous volutes, it is the principal decorative element of the facade.*

The main house and chapel atop the terrace at Savonet. The raised platform overlooks much of the estate.

The Chobolobo residence at Willemstad. The walls are simple, almost bare, and yet the gable and its accompanying volutes—which immediately give away their derivation—are very evocative.

*Overleaf:
Two perfectly preserved gables at Oranjestad, capital of the island of Aruba.*

A gabled facade on Aruba. The forms, colors, and decorations of the gables are always distinctive.

The Governor's Palace on Aruba, which displays both Portuguese and Dutch influences. It stands in the center of Oranjestad, surrounded by a small garden.

Right:
A window composition combining European form and Caribbean color.

Far right:
Groot Kwartier on Curaçao, which has a Dutch color scheme. The triangular motifs that flank the entrance seem to have been derived from castles on the polders.

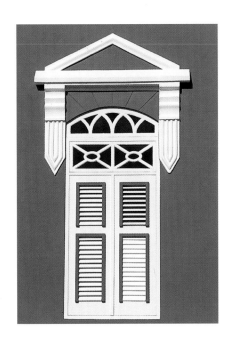

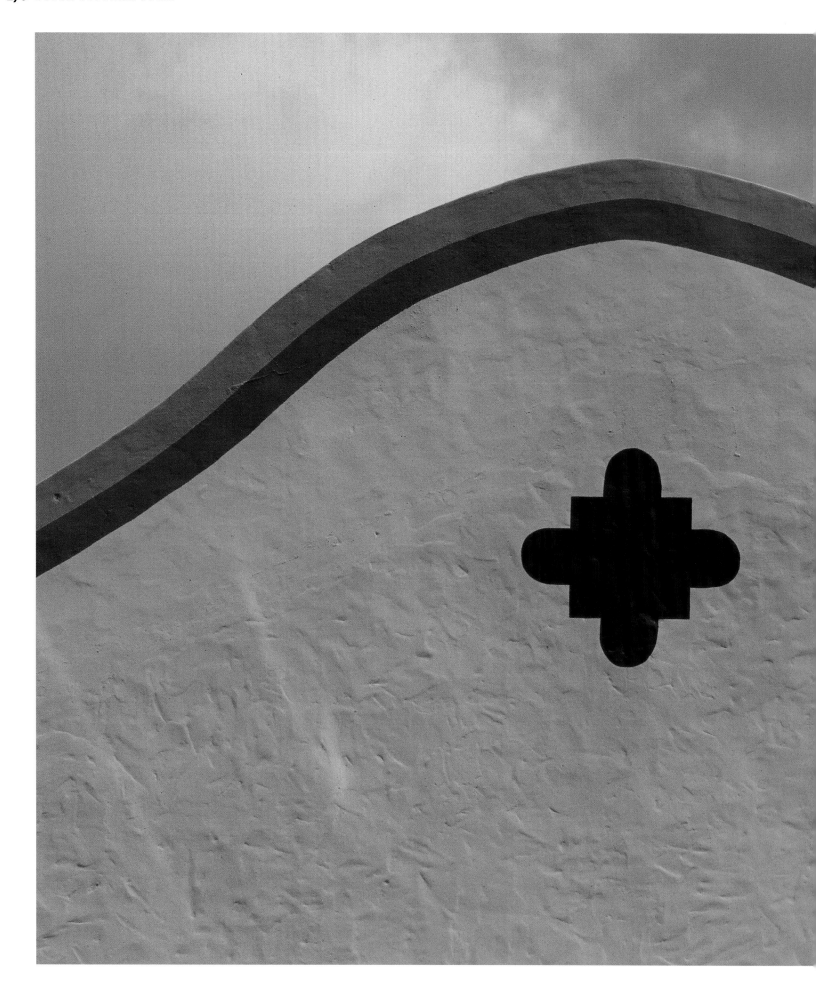

Top:
Dormer window on
Aruba.

Above:
Dormer window on
Curaçao. Such elements
both illuminated the
attic floor and also
served as a defining
characteristic of Dutch
colonial architecture.

A broad curved
pediment on Saint
Martin.

The Cape Dutch Style

South Africa

At the southern tip of the continent, celebrated for its pleasant climate and aromatic wines, stand the homes of the Boers, the Dutch settlers who occupied the land from the seventeenth century onward. The region is characterized by attention to detail, cunning exploitation of materials, and successful insertion of the architecture into the beautiful setting.

The soil in the Cape area is extremely fertile, the climate is mild all year round, and the surrounding views are dominated by gentle slopes, on which rows of vines trace abstract geometrical patterns. Here, in 1717, Hermanus Bosman founded the Nieuwe Platatie, or "New Plantation," where he built a modest house flanked by a series of outbuildings. After 1770 the main house was enlarged and assumed the austere yet graceful appearance of so many farmhouses built in the Cape Dutch style.

Simple and usually whitewashed, Afrikaans residences feature elaborate pediments and gables made up of a series of volutes; the date of construction was frequently carved on the gable, which sets them apart and makes them immediately recognizable. The gardens are striking for the varieties of plants they contain and especially for the size and shape attained by some species, which in Europe can only survive indoors.

In spite of their shared history, various regions offer differences in style. In, for example, Johannesburg or Durban, the Cape Dutch style is mixed with Victorian citations, introduced during the brief period of British rule. As is true of many of the distant lands colonized by Europeans, the intermingling of two or more cultures results in a style that is perhaps less pure but significantly richer.

The elegant drawing room of Groot Libertas, near Stellenbosch in the Cape Town area. The majority of Boers in the region made their fortune by planting vineyards.

The walls of Groot Libertas, decorated with delicate paintings. Many of the original furnishings have been preserved.

Melrose House in Pretoria. Although located far from the original Boer settlements, the residence is nevertheless in the Cape Dutch style.

Grande Roche, a farm at Paarl, made up of the main house and various annexes. Set against a splendid natural backdrop, the complex, now a hotel, is still surrounded by carefully tended vineyards.

The Boschendal farm, in the area of Franschhoek, a small town set among vineyards in the Cape region. Boschendal is one of the most interesting farms in the area.

The main entrance of Grande Roche, at Paarl. The restoration maintained the building's original characteristics and decoration.

Overleaf:
The lake in front of Vergelegen. The Stellenbosch area is one of the most fertile in South Africa—and, not coincidentally, the place where the first colonists settled.

*Farmhouse on the Cape.
Such structures typically
have a single story with
a mansard above.*

*House on a farm on the
Cape. Four pediments
with windows serve to
illuminate the attic floor.*

The oldest building at Vergelegen. It is thatched with straw, which must be renewed regularly. The farm is located near Stellenbosch, the wine-producing region near Cape Town.

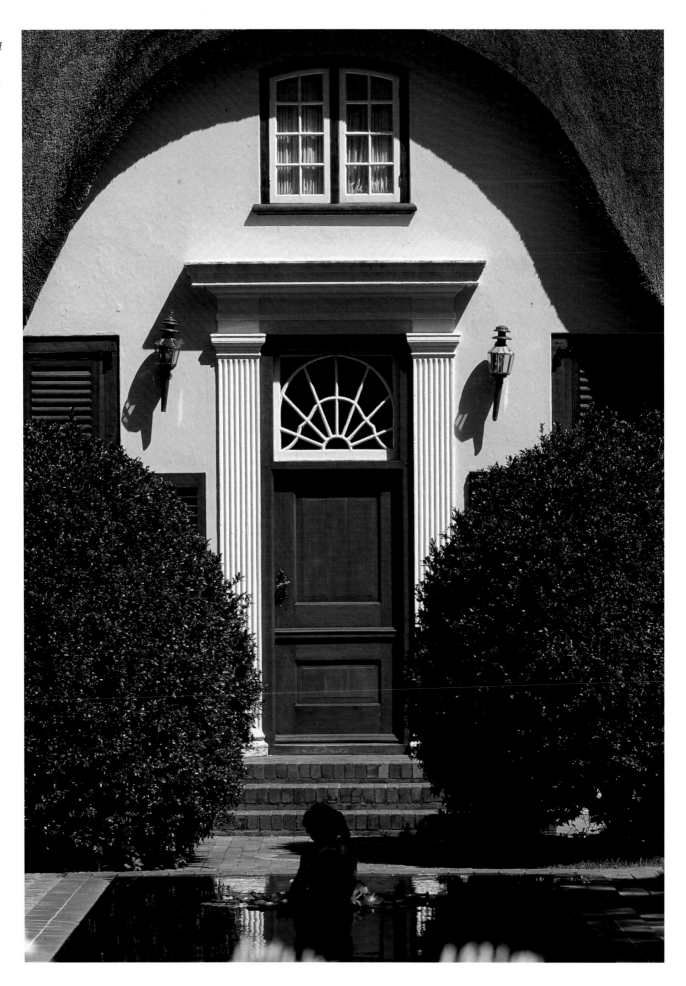

Below:
The drawing room at Groot Constantia. Many of the early houses, stately in form, were rather spartan in their furnishings.

Bottom:
A bedroom at Groot Constantia. Wealthier colonists had furniture sent out from their home countries, while others used locally made replicas.

Groot Constantia, one of the oldest and best-known farms in South Africa. One of the first to produce wine, it is today open to visitors.

The pediment on the cellar at Groot Constantia. Each of the outbuildings, though somewhat small, is decorated with tympana, volutes, statues, and stuccoes.

A house at the Vergelegen complex, Stellenbosch, framed by majestic camphor trees.

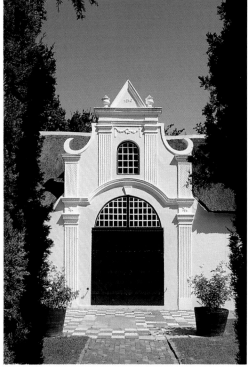

*Far left:
Pediment in the Cape Dutch style at the Boschendal house at Franschhoek, which frames the entrance to a cellar.*

*Left:
Pediment at Vergelegen, at Stellenbosch, over the entrance to a library.*

A farm at Paarl surrounded by vineyards and mountains.

In the Shadow of the Company

Capital at the sultan's palace at Yogyakarta. When the Dutch occupied Indonesia they offered a ceremonial *role to the sultans, leading to a regular cultural and artistic exchange between the two peoples.*

Also known as the Paradise Island, Bali symbolizes Indonesia for the West. It is one of the most beautiful islands in the archipelago and still retains its most fascinating qualities. Since ancient times its fertile soil has made it a privileged oasis covered with rice paddies, the emerald green enlivened by the brilliant colors of the local textiles.

Bali is the only island in the area not to have been converted to Islam: the migration of Javanese nobility and priests, who in the sixteenth century took refuge there from the advance of Islam, has made it a stronghold of Hinduism. In front of each house is a small temple to the gods, and a peaceful and tolerant atmosphere reigns. Since benign spirits are believed to live in the mountains and evil ones at the bottom of the sea, the ideal place to build a house is on a hillside, and the most interesting residences on the island are indeed on the slopes of Bali's three mountains.

The typical pattern of settlement on Bali is a complex that houses the various families of a clan in small, separate buildings surrounded by an enclosure and arranged around a bale, a pavilion set in the middle of the assemblage that is used for both meetings and entertainment. The patriarch's residence is the largest and most ornately decorated. All of the houses feature a patio that is an integral part of the living space and is furnished as if it were an interior.

The Portuguese discovered such complexes when then arrived on the island at the beginning of the sixteenth century, as did the Dutch at the end of the century. The Dutch were quick to grasp the economic potential of these lands and in 1602 founded the East India Company, which played a fundamental role in the development of the Indonesian archipelago.

The arrival of Europeans brought about a fusion of architectural traditions. The Dutch, in recognition of the profound differences in climate between the two countries, redesigned their houses so that they opened onto large patios. The typical gables of Dutch buildings were blended with the forms and colors indigenous to the island. In fact, there are few other former European colonies where the local architectural tradition has survived as intact as it has here.

A pronaos at the entrance to a pavilion in the sultan's palace at Yogyakarta. The pediment has Dutch forms but is decorated in the Indonesian style.

Unusual motifs on the tympanum of a Surakarta residence, on the island of Java.

A pavilion at Yogyakarta. The structure is open; the roof hints at the form of a fretwork wooden gable.

The open-air ballroom of the sultan's palace at Yogyakarta.

The kraton, or palace of the sultan, at Surakarta. The many spaces open at the sides are a direct consequence of the constant humidity and high temperatures.

The entrance to the sultan's palace at Yogyakarta. The tympanum, frieze, and coupled columns are drawn from the classical tradition of Europe, but the decorations and colors are indigenous.

A miniature pronaos over the entrance to an annex of the sultan's palace.

Residence on Bali. The influence of the Dutch was less powerful than on Java.

Left:
A typically Indonesian roof at Karangasem on Bali.

Right:
A Karangasem building with elements drawn from European architecture.

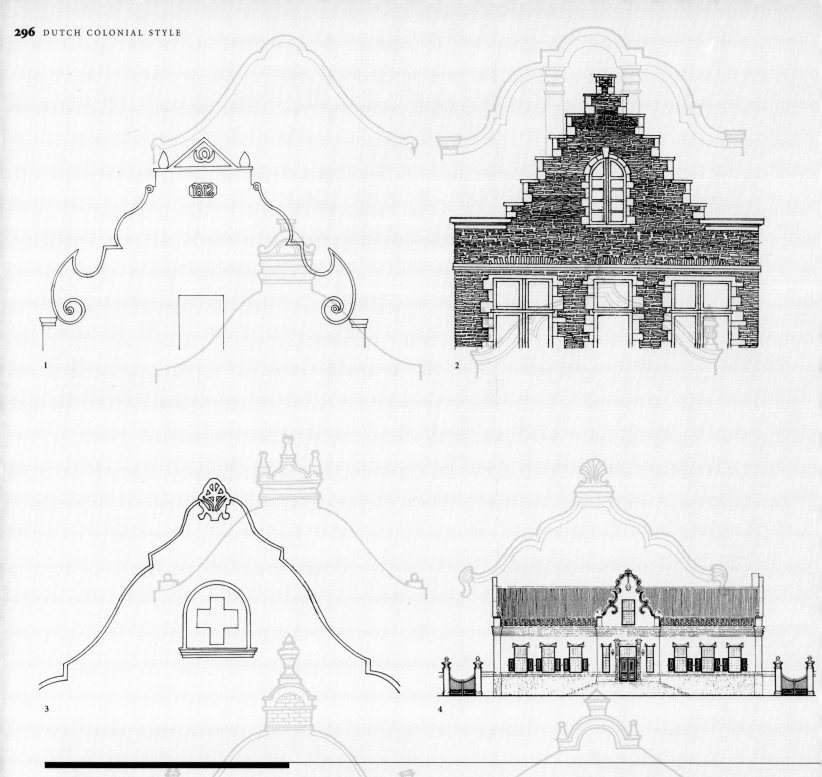

1

2

3

4

AN EXALTATION OF
PEDIMENTS AND GABLES

The importance of the pediment as an element of classical design has led architects of different ages to invent new combinations and variations. This process reached its height in baroque and rococo buildings, before neoclassical sobriety prompted a return to simpler forms.

Pediments are often broken at the top, in order to house an object. The pediment was seen as the ideal location to place a bust, statue, urn, or other decorative or symbolic sculpture. The space on the facade between the pitches of the roof is the natural location for the pediment. When it fills the space between two stories a window is often set within it, and this may be in turn surmounted by another pediment.

Baroque architects took this decorative and formal element from classical architecture and transformed it: they expanded, broke, and elongated it, giving it entirely new shapes, proportions, and positions. When the situation and the available materials required, it could even be left without moldings and other secondary elements. In the countries of Northern Europe overlapping flat clay tiles were well suited to covering steeply pitched roofs. In the seventeenth century, architects showed remarkable ingenuity in adapting classical pediments derived from Mediterranean buildings with flatter pitches to the facades that resulted from the use of more steeply sloping ones in the north. A great number of variations on these features was developed to adapt them to the new spaces. Yet the importance given to the pediment and the gables is such that their identity is still apparent even when they are reduced to a few distorted elements. In the Netherlands and its colonies, pediments and gables built out of brick and stone and covered with whitewashed stucco and plaster have always been used to give a dignified appearance to buildings and to draw attention to their distinctive facades.

6

1. *A pediment at Vergelegen, near Stellenbosch.*

2. *The front of a townhouse in Amsterdam, with a stepped tympanum.*

3. *A cruciform window in a mansard in the Cape region.*

4. *Facade of a typical South African farmhouse.*

5. *A South African farmhouse with an unusual T-shaped plan.*

6. *An elaborate pediment topped by an aedicule, an adaptation of a typical Dutch townhouse composition. The volutes are inserted between plaster partitions.*

Ottoman Colonial Style

The Ottoman empire was one of the longest-lived of the second millennium. Established in the fourteenth century, it survived until 1924, when it was dissolved to make way for the present Turkish republic.

The golden age of the empire stretched from the fall of Constantinople in 1453 to the death of Suleiman the Magnificent in 1566. In this period a new artistic style developed that blended Byzantine and Hellenistic influences with Islamic art.

This artistic flowering is most evident in the mosques, but it also found expression in caravanserais, *hammams* (the celebrated Turkish baths), and fountains placed in the center of gardens and houses. The most important symbol of Ottoman residential architecture is the Topkapi Saray in Istanbul, one of the finest such buildings in the entire Islamic world.

Ottoman cities were not planned. Neighborhoods sprang up spontaneously and were surrounded by open spaces. In the last years of the empire, toward the end of the nineteenth century, the architecture started to come under the influence of European styles, in particular the baroque and neoclassical. The marks left by Ottoman rule are evident from Poland to Romania and from Greece to the Middle East and Egypt.

At Home with the Viziers

Preceding pages:
The courtyard of
Bayt 'Azm palace, at
Hamah, Syria.

Below:
A decorative panel with
motifs typical of Islamic
art.

The difficulty of defining a Middle Eastern style is evident from the cities of the region, with their many and varied peoples and cultures that have helped to shape and enrich the architectural tradition of these lands. Arab, Ottoman, Mameluke, British, French, German, and Russian influences are coupled with the omnipresent local pink stone that characterizes nearly every construction.

The earliest upper-class residences in Damascus and Jerusalem date from the sixteenth to seventeenth centuries, the Mameluke period, which coincided with a great flowering of the arts. After an eighteenth-century decline, the region was revitalized in the nineteenth. Many elegant houses were built by Arab merchants, and the first Jewish area was established outside the walls of Jerusalem. Arab settlements differed from Jewish ones in the haphazard nature of their layout: each builder was free to choose the shape of the lot and the orientation of the house, and would construct the road that led to it.

The mixture of forms and styles is most evident in the decorations. These are largely geometric and sometimes take the form of inscriptions but are hardly ever figurative, since the Koran forbids the representation of living creatures. Often windows in the Renaissance style alternate with tympana supported by slender pillars. The simplicity of the exterior contrasts with particularly sumptuous interiors, with elegant wooden ceilings decorated with fine paintings. Armenian glazed terra-cotta tiles, usually in various shades of blue, are omnipresent. The Middle East—cradle of ancient civilizations, crossroads of cultures and religions—is a unique kaleidoscope of races and styles, where indigenous peoples, colonizers, and immigrants have each made their own contribution.

A projecting window
with an unusual curved
grating in Arab Jerusalem.
The composition is
crowned with a broken
tympanum.

A large neo-baroque
residence on the road
between Jerusalem and
Bethlehem. A broad
curved staircase with two
flights of steps leads to
the main floor.

Two-story portico in
Jerusalem. It is built
out of the pink stone
used for almost all the
buildings in the city.

Above:
The large courtyard of
the Sebai palace in the
center of Damascus,
with various plants
and a fountain in the
middle. The floor
and walls are covered
with polychrome tiles.

Right:
A corner of the Sebai
palace. The forms and
decorations are typical
of those imported when
the country was under
Ottoman rule.

Overleaf top left:
A room opening onto
the courtyard of the
Ajakbash palace in
Aleppo.

Overleaf bottom left:
A large portal in
Damascus. The pillars
are decorated with fine
marble inlays.

Overleaf right:
Windows looking onto
the courtyard of the
Ajakbash palace in
Aleppo.

Orient House, one of the most interesting Arab residences in Jerusalem. Both Ottoman and British influences are evident.

The gallery of a palace in Jerusalem, which stands on slender coupled columns. White stone was rarely used, while pink stone was common. Occasionally, they were used together to create an attractive contrast.

*A fine wooden ceiling
decorated with paintings
in a palace in Damascus.*

*Right:
Vaulted rooms of a
residence in Damascus.
Increasing the volume
of interior spaces helped
keep them cool.*

*Far right:
An interior at Anbar
palace in Damascus.*

A residence formerly belonging to an Arab or Turkish merchant in the Arab quarter of Jerusalem.

Bayt 'Azm palace, at Hamah. A vast complex, it is made up of several different buildings. The two-color stone decoration of the arches is a characteristic feature.

Small shrine at the center of a garden in Aleppo, Syria.

ISLAMIC FORMS

Repetition is the most obvious principle of Islamic decorative art. Recurring patterns are derived from a limited number of basic formulas: geometric shapes, calligraphy, floral and other figurative motifs, and arabesques. Islamic art inherited geometric patterns from the late classical world but took them to an unprecedented level of complexity, drawing inspiration from the principles of symmetry and repetition that had been uncovered by Arab mathematicians.

The geometric schemes that form the basis of the decorative elements are independent of scale and may be applied to a wide variety of materials; they allow a relationship to be established between the different parts of a building, both inside and out. The basic form is the circle, and the length of its radius determines the proportions. This basic unit can be developed into a square, a triangle, or any other polygon. One of the most common geometric shapes is the six- or sixteen-pointed star.

In the Islamic world this endless iteration of geometric patterns is interpreted as a visual manifestation of God, representing unity in multiplicity and multiplicity in unity. However, geometric compositions are just one form of Islamic art. Calligraphic decoration, which may be integrated with geometric designs, is considered one of the highest forms of art since it reproduces the word of God. Inscriptions on buildings are generally in the sober Kufic style or in the later, more cursive *naskhi* and its varieties, such as *thuluth*. The variations change from region to region and century to century.

The arabesque is the other major element of Islamic decorative architecture. It is governed by mathematical principles that generate complex geometric shapes. The forms of the arabesque evolved in the face of European cultural influences, particularly the medieval and baroque. Europe was also fascinated by the evolution of these forms; Vasari refers to something similar to the arabesque in his *Lives*, though he called it *damaschina* after its presumed place of origin, Damascus.

1. Window in a Muslim house, screened to ensure privacy.

2. Decorative calligraphy, frequently used in Islamic architecture.

3. Horseshoe-shaped window.

4. Column capital in Jerusalem.

5. A geometric decorative motif.

6. Column capital decorated with floral motifs.

7. Wind tower, used to increase ventilation.

8. Wind tower.

9. Doorway with a pointed arch.

10. Geometrical patterns carved in bas-relief, used to decorate the walls of Arab buildings.

11. Window decorated with an elegant pediment.

12. Small tower topped by an onion dome.

13. Example of calligraphic decoration.

14. Four-light window with composite arches.

In 1644 the Ming dynasty was overthrown by the Manchu who, after expanding their territory as far as the Great Wall and their influence over the whole of China, conquered Beijing and took power as the Ch'ing dynasty. Under its rule China expanded and experienced a period of remarkable prosperity and stability.

Korea was reduced to vassal status in 1637, while Taiwan, occupied by the Ming in 1662, was finally conquered by the Ch'ing in 1683. By 1820 China was the largest and most populous empire in the world. It controlled a huge expanse of Central Asia as well as regions including Korea, Indochina, Siam, Burma, and Nepal.

When the Europeans arrived at the end of the nineteenth century, with their technological and organizational superiority and determination to establish trade links with this part of the world, the court in Beijing, by then corrupt and decadent, underestimated the threat they posed. Discord, revolts, wars, and insurrections brought matters to a head.

A republic was proclaimed on January 1, 1912. It was the end of an empire that had been the master of the East since the time of Marco Polo. Yet its culture and its art were not destroyed and survive to this day, even in the territories that it conquered.

In the Hermit Kingdom

It was not until 1883 that Korea, the so-called Hermit Kingdom, the "Land of Morning Peace," opened its frontiers. Perhaps the influence of the Chinese and Japanese had counseled prudence and the country's sages, unwilling to compromise and determined to preserve their cultural identity intact, had preferred to avoid contact with the outside world.

Korean residential complexes are generally laid out around one or more rectangular courtyards bounded by service buildings; the main house is at the center. Often the main house is ringed by other dwellings used by members of the same clan and arranged in a strict hierarchy. Tall outer walls, embellished with elegant Greek frets and other geometrical patterns, defend these ancient examples of residential life.

The atmosphere consists of colors, subtle nuances, and religious and astrological symbols. The clearly identifiable external influences, especially those of China, do not mar the stylistic unity of Korean palaces and pavilions. The superimposed, curved roofs, rendered waterproof by a layer of clay-and-straw mortar on top of wooden boards, are highly reminiscent of those in China, but the characteristic series of attics set one on top of the other (the "Korean pavilion"), the way some rooms are raised on stone pillars, the use of carved and painted wood, and the form and arrangement of the *chapsang* (the clay "guardians" that protect houses) testify to the originality of the indigenous architecture.

Numerous patios are supported by square wooden pillars connected to the lintels by simple capitals. Openings are large, many of them covered by carved wooden jalousies as fine as lace. In fact the working of wood, in this land of forests, is a widespread and ancient tradition that has led to the development of sophisticated structures, often constructed without the use of nails.

Preceding pages:
Chongmyo Shrine in
Seoul.

Below:
The wall of a Korean
garden. By tradition, the
outside wall is decorated
in the same way as those
of the house itself.

A patio at Pulguksa,
Kyŏngju. Beams and
columns of painted wood
are the most common
decoration in Korea.

Pavilion in the Chikjsa
complex, at Taegu in the
northern part of South
Korea.

A building in Taegu.
Slats of wood interlaced
in various patterns screen
the wall, maintaining
the occupants' privacy
while allowing views out.

A portico at Chongmyo Shrine. Wood and stone are the most commonly used materials in the old buildings of Seoul.

Lavishly ornamented eaves on a residence. The structure of the eaves, distinctive because of its upward tilt, is often the most important part of a building's decoration.

Wooden pavilions at Suwŏn, which stand on stone piles.

One of the oldest
buildings in Angang,
constructed out of wood.
The complex, called
Oksan, is made up of
several houses
surrounded by an
outer wall.

The simple but elegant
front of a house in the
Popchusa, at Poun.

Beautiful Island

Taiwan

A watercolor by Li Sung, an artist of the Sung dynasty. Painted at the beginning of the thirteenth century, it depicts a Chinese house by the sea on Taiwan.

Ilha formosa! cried seventeenth-century Portuguese sailors as they passed the island on their way to Japan. "Beautiful island" was a name that remained in use among Europeans for a long time, while people in the East called it T'ai-wan. Such beauty tempted many to try to take possession of the island, Chinese, European, and Japanese. The oldest Chinese document referring to Taiwan dates from 206 BCE, and the first attempt at conquest took place four centuries later. During the Ming dynasty in the fourteenth through seventeenth centuries, increasing numbers of Chinese moved to the island, which had become a haven for plunderers, pirates, and unscrupulous merchants. Its position close to the trade routes of China and Japan and the lack of controls made it a free and ungoverned port.

Only with the exodus from the mainland that occurred after Chiang Kai-shek set up the Nationalist government in exile on the island did it become truly Chinese. But the architecture had always been Chinese. The style is classical, with lacquered wood, graceful forms, and sloping roofs. The houses of the nobility and bourgeoisie stood inside enclosures and were often set in formal gardens dotted with pavilions and circular doorways. Views were carefully studied, for the Chinese dwelling was supposed to be a place of repose for the spirit as well as the body. Water, a symbol of life and serenity, was present in pools and small channels. Low walls alternated typical round openings with open spaces, also in the Chinese manner. Taiwan, apart from a brief period of Japanese rule, has always remained within the orbit of Chinese culture and history.

Ta-shi Tse Hu, the country residence of Chiang Kai-shek, founder of the modern state of Taiwan. It has been turned into a mausoleum.

Top:
The entrance to an
upper-class residence
in Taipei.

Above:
The boundary wall of
an estate in Taipei. The
stylistic features are
typical of mainland
Chinese architecture.

A typical roof in Taipei.
Conical roofs terminating
in spires are a recurrent
motif in Chinese
architecture.

*A pavilion facing a lily
pond in the Lin garden,
at Taipei. Wealthy
families always set their
homes in gardens, even
in the city.*

*Chuen Chiu at
Kao-hsiung, in the far
south of the island.
Various buildings with
porticoes face a large
courtyard.*

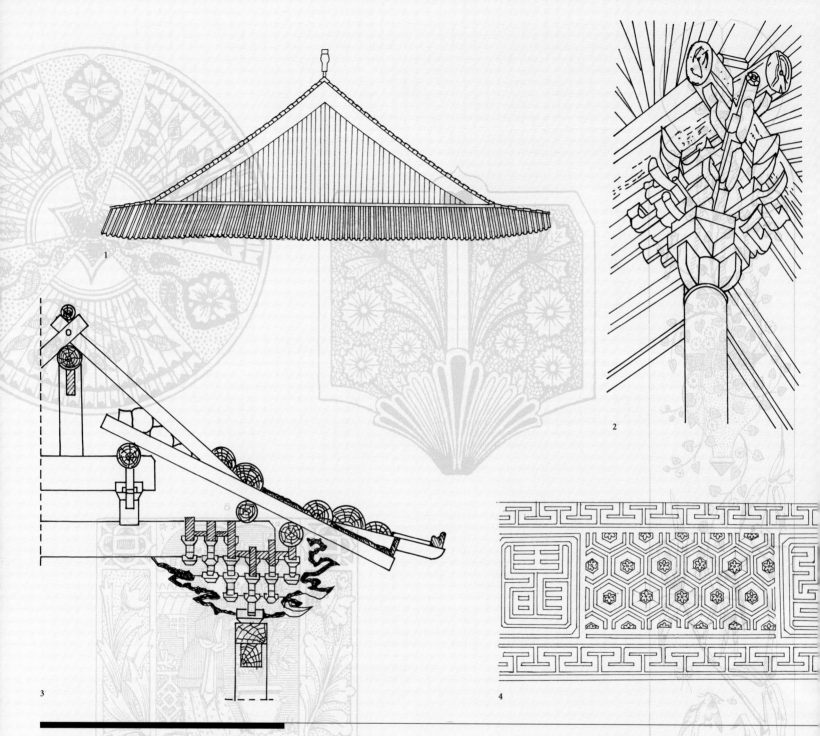

1

2

3

4

AMONG THE TURNED-UP ROOFS

Since ancient times Chinese architecture has been characterized by a layout based around a central room. Originally these rooms were bounded by wooden pillars standing on stone bases, while the floor was made of beaten earth. The roof, the building's most distinctive feature, was usually covered by tiles; the color of the tiles identified the social status of the owner. This covering could take the form of a hip or saddle roof, or it could be a combination of different types. The eaves were raised at the corners, giving them their typical "turned-up" appearance.

Small rafters added to the main beams of the roof at different angles intensified the effect.

Over the centuries and under a series of dynasties the structural system was refined. Inside and outside walls became lighter, eventually turning into little more than screens. The task of supporting the structure was given to the pillars and beams. Different colors identified the different functions of the architectural members. The supporting framework was usually painted red, while the ends of the beams were painted in bright and highly contrasting shades.

The central room was surrounded by an open gallery covered by the eaves. Ceilings were flat, coffered, or raised like a canopy. Interiors were relatively simple. The largest residential complexes consisted of

a series of halls facing onto courtyards. These were bounded by corridors and outbuildings, while gardens and pools of water were located at the center.

Although the Chinese style of architecture has come under the influence of distant cultures—from Persia to India—at various times, it has remained relatively pure. It was not until the establishment of the republic, in 1912, that European styles began to make an impact, though they were still reinterpreted in the light of local tradition.

1. A pediment of the Kyong palace, Yi dynasty, in Korea.

2. Detail of the complex system of joints in a roof.

3. Section through the junction between the supporting structure and the roof.

4. Tall stone wall enclosing a residential complex in Seoul.

5. Yongkyongdoig, an ancient Chinese residential complex. The service buildings are arranged along the edges of the property while the main house is at the center.

6. Ch'angdokkung, a family village, surrounded by open space.

7. The residential complex of a clan.

Italian Colonial Style

The Italian colonial adventure got off to a late start, at the turn of the twentieth century, and was only consolidated in the period between the two world wars. Italy's overseas territories were located in Africa and in the Balkans. Eritrea was occupied first, and then Somalia, Libya, and finally Albania and Ethiopia; defeat in Ethiopia scuttled all dreams of expansion.

A stay of a few decades was not enough to leave a deep mark on the local architecture and city planning, and in Africa the Italians colonized territories that had previously been within the British or Arab sphere of influence. These factors may have contributed to making Italian colonial style yet another hybrid, the outcome of a difficult juggling act between local tradition, the British Victorian style, neoclassicism, the modern movement, and the arabesques and pointed arches of Islamic derivation. Nonetheless, the Italians did a great deal of building, especially in Eritrea and Somalia, though little of it remains today. Wars, revolutions, and neglect have greatly altered or destroyed many of these buildings, and those that do survive do not represent a coherent style of colonial architecture but rather an architecture that is the fruit of a whole range of influences, compromises, and creative impulses.

"A Place in the Sun"

East Africa

Preceding pages:
A building in the Piazza
area of Addis Ababa. The
region was given this
name during the brief
Italian occupation.

Below:
A Coptic cross at
Aksum in Ethiopia, in
the vicinity of Adwa.

In 1869 the Genoese shipowner Raffaello Rubattino acquired the Bay of Aseb in Eritrea through the offices of the former missionary Giuseppe Sapeto. The sellers were the sultans Ibrahim and Hassan Ben Ahmed of Afar. A few years later Rubattini sold the area to the Italian state, which was looking for what the rhetoric of the Fascist regime would later define as "a place in the sun." Though chiefly a question of prestige, the acquisition was also motivated by the desire to vie with the French port of Djibouti, which had long controlled trade in the Red Sea. Immediately afterward the Italian state dispatched soldiers and a group of functionaries to Eritrea. It also occupied Massawa, formed alliances with local leaders, who were frequently feuding with one another, and finally, in 1890, decreed the unification of the "Italian possessions on the Red Sea." Thus Italy's first colony on African territory was born.

Few people were prepared to move to the colony, and the lack of Italian civilians meant that very little was built. With the rise of Mussolini, interest in the overseas territory was revived. The number of settlers rose rapidly and soon reached sixty thousand. The colony of Italian East Africa comprised the modern states of Eritrea, Ethiopia, and Somalia; its main cities were Massawa, Addis Ababa, Mogadishu, and the settlement known as Duca degli Abruzzi, constructed to the north of the Somali capital and intended exclusively for colonists.

The most fertile period for colonial building was the two decades of Fascist rule. The early stone constructions were joined by new brick and wood ones, especially after the technology for industrial production of the components had been refined. Most of the houses had large balconies and wooden columns and capitals, along with roofs of corrugated iron, which were cheap but devoid of insulation. The vernacular style of architecture was combined with those of Europe (both Italian and British) and the avant-garde modern movement. The result was eclectic: baroque and neoclassical pediments, neo-Renaissance and Victorian facades, curved and bare walls that echoed Gropius and Le Corbusier.

The beginning of World War II marked the end of this brief interlude. In 1941 the British occupied Eritrea and liberated the other territories that had been annexed, and the birth of three independent states soon followed.

An example of Italian
architecture at Aksum.
Pilasters and capitals
have been freely reworked
and reassembled.

The neoclassical pronaos of Villa Rasnadew at Addis Ababa.

A long open gallery at Addis Ababa. It serves the rooms facing the courtyard, the site of a simple garden.

A Renaissance-inspired
villa, built in the 1930s
at Aksum in the north
of Ethiopia, close to the
border with Eritrea.

Volute on the corner of
a building at Aksum.

Sheik Ojelle, one of the most important and elegant mansions in Addis Ababa. Many of its structures are built out of wood. The building is used as a school.

A wooden balcony at Ras Seyoum, a colonial building in the Ethiopian capital.

Ras Biru's house, standing surrounded by a garden on a terrace in the center of Addis Ababa, just a short distance from the park of the presidential palace. The glassed-in balcony offers a magnificent view of the city.

Opposite top:
Wall decoration on
the facade of an Italian
residence in Addis
Ababa.

Opposite bottom:
The multicolored arch
of a neoclassical building
in the Mercato quarter
of the city. The district
received its name during
the Italian period.

Below:
Turret with a mixtilinear
roof, over a belvedere at
Ras Biru's house. Such
turrets were built by the
British.

Right:
A turret, used as a
drawing room, in Addis
Ababa.

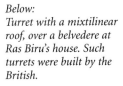

Turret set at the corner of an estate at Aksum, in the north of Ethiopia. The architectural traditions of the region have always been strong; British and Italian influences were merely grafted onto them.

Far left and left: Windows at Aksum. Color helps to alleviate the monotonous gray tint of the stone.

A building at Aksum.
Though constructed
of local materials, it
displays foreign
influences.

Italian Renaissance–
style villa in the Piazza
quarter of the Ethiopian
capital.

Classically inspired
residence—with
indigenous influences—
in the Piazza quarter.

*A gleaming white villa
on Lido Avenue in
Mogadishu, Somalia.*

*An Italian house in
Mogadishu, on Avenue
of the United Nations.
The parapet of the stairs
features fine baroque
volutes.*

House fusing Italian and local styles. During the twenty years of Fascist rule, Italian colonial architecture reached its peak.

A colonial house in a new residential neighborhood in Somalia, surrounded by a garden.

A building in the Duca degli Abruzzi village in Somalia.

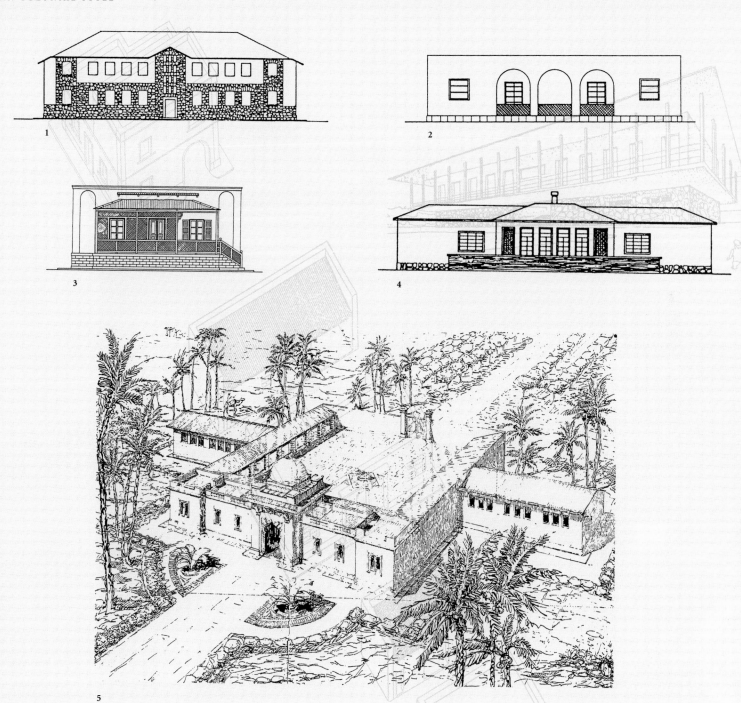

1

2

3

4

5

CLASSICAL AND FUTURIST STATELINESS

In the Ethiopia of the 1920s and 1930s, while buildings were still being constructed on a central plan in the age-old manner of the kingdom of the Negus, rationalist architecture was imported from Italy. Although the colonists were obliged, for economic reasons, to use local materials, their new homes still bore the mark of the European tradition of architecture. By the time Italians arrived in large numbers between the two world wars, there already existed a hybrid style of architecture, created by the dominant Shewan ethnic group, which had come into contact with the British and started to adopt some of their ways.

The walls of the Italian buildings were constructed out of rough stone, with dressed stone or locally produced brick used for corners and jambs. The roofs had steep pitches and eaves that overhung the edges of the buildings. The masonry, whether of brick or stone, was left visible, and wherever possible, a wooden verandah was inserted (an element that proved indispensable in the hot and humid regions of the plains). These were at once the characteristic and the outstanding features of colonial architecture in Italy's overseas possessions.

However, different tendencies emerged in different regions. In Eritrea, for example, and especially at Asmara, there were more buildings in the style of the Italian modernists, since the city was linked by rail to the port of Massawa and it was possible to bring construction materials like cement and steel from Italy. In Ethiopia, on the other hand, traditional structures persisted for a longer time, notably those with a circular plan typical of indigenous architecture, a design that was used for Coptic churches as well as for dwellings.

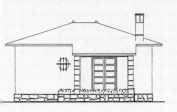

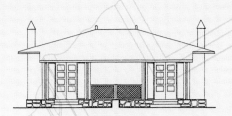

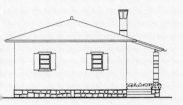

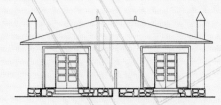

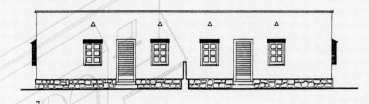

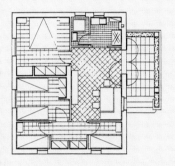

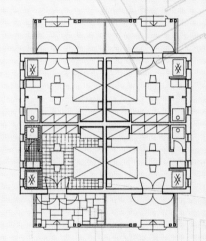

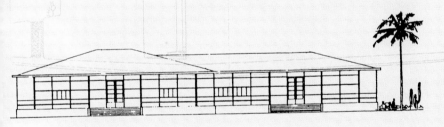

1. Large residence designed for the East African colonies.

2. Single-family house in Tripolitania.

3. Single-family house.

4. Single-family residence.

5. A Libyan mansion on a plantation.

6. Elevations and plans of houses for the Italian colonies.

7. Study of a prefabricated house for the Autonomous Fascist Institute of Low-Rent Housing.

8. Residence for an Italian functionary in Mogadishu, c. 1930.

9. A prefabricated house that can be dismantled, designed in the 1930s especially for tropical climates.

The scent of sandalwood fills
the air around the majestic
forts of Oman, an ancient
sultanate with a lively artistic
tradition. Even in Roman
times the Omanis were
known for their trade in
incense and myrrh. Later
came the period of great date
and banana plantations and
stock farms. In the eighteenth
century the sultanate began
to expand overseas, acquiring
territory in Africa first, on
the coasts of Kenya and the
island of Zanzibar, and on
the Indian subcontinent, on
the west coast of modern
India, and the south coast of
what is now Pakistan.

In the seventeenth and
eighteenth centuries Omani
merchants traded spices
and slaves, chiefly with the
Portuguese, who used to stop
at Zanzibar on their way to
the East Indies. Later, as the
British put pressure on the
Omanis to sign treaties of
protection and the territory
was divided up among
various sultans, powerful
fortified dwellings were constructed both at home and
in the African possessions.

The sumptuous residences
built in the sultanate's
African colonies still have elegant portals of inlaid wood,
decorated with auspicious
inscriptions from the Koran.
They are unquestionably the
finest testimonies to Oman's
colonial period.

On the Island of Spices

The small island that lies off Dar es Salaam was one of the first European settlements established on the route to the East Indies, along with those of Mombasa and the nearby island of Pemba. The Portuguese first grasped the crucial importance of the place, transforming it into an important trade center after Vasco da Gama's voyage of exploration. The island's strategic position, especially in relation to the monsoon winds that governed the movement of ships, attracted merchants from India and the countries of Arabia, in particular the sultanate of Oman. By the middle of the seventeenth century Zanzibar was in Omani hands and gradually developed into a major market for the slaves that were needed to run plantations in the East Indies.

The Omanis established an ever firmer grip on the island. In the first half of the nineteenth century so many wealthy Arab traders moved there that the sultan of Oman decided to make it his new capital. It then went through a series of political vicissitudes, influenced by international and especially European diplomacy, until becoming a British protectorate toward the end of the century.

The buildings, their decorations, and above all the finely inlaid doors testify to a wide variety of periods, tastes, and cultures. Doorways became the chief mode of expression for residential architecture: vaulted, architraved, and with one or two openings, they still represent the principal status symbol of the owner, used to communicate nationality, culture, and social origin. Large brass knobs and studs both strengthen and decorate the doors, and almost obsessive attention is devoted to each functional element. It is the entrances, more than the houses and palaces, that determine the character of Stone Town, the old part of Zanzibar. In this enclosed area, the original nucleus of the city, the legendary island of spices still displays the glories of its past.

Preceding pages:
The tympanum of a
finely carved portal on
Zanzibar.

Below:
The system used to
lock the island's doors.

The patio of Tembo
House, a mansion in the
center of Stone Town. It
is only a short distance
from the beach.

The sultan's palace on Zanzibar, one of the most fascinating residences built by the Omanis.

Interior of the sultan's palace. Each room is richly decorated in the Omani style.

Far left and left: Doors fortified with heavy studs and embellished with fine inlays.

Brass studs, one of the most typical features of the doors on Zanzibar. According to tradition, they were originally set on the doors of forts to prevent elephants being used to break them down.

An engraved brass door knocker.

Two simple leaves of a door in a rich and elegant frame.

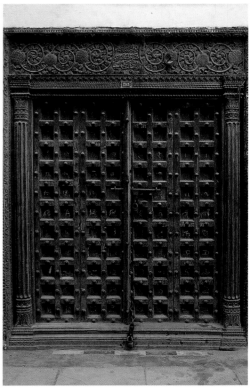

A paneled door framed by fluted half-columns.

One of the finest buildings on Zanzibar. The architecture consists of Omani, African, and, above all, British influences.

A column capital on the Zanzibar structure. A recent restoration has brought the building back to its original glory.

A building just outside the historic center of the capital blending Omani and British influences.

A residence, recently converted into a hotel, set in a garden of palm trees.

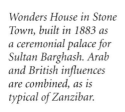

Wonders House in Stone Town, built in 1883 as a ceremonial palace for Sultan Barghash. Arab and British influences are combined, as is typical of Zanzibar.

Balconies on a Zanzibar residence. The long balcony is located on the third floor of the building; the second floor has screened windows.

Second-floor balcony on a dwelling in Zanzibar.

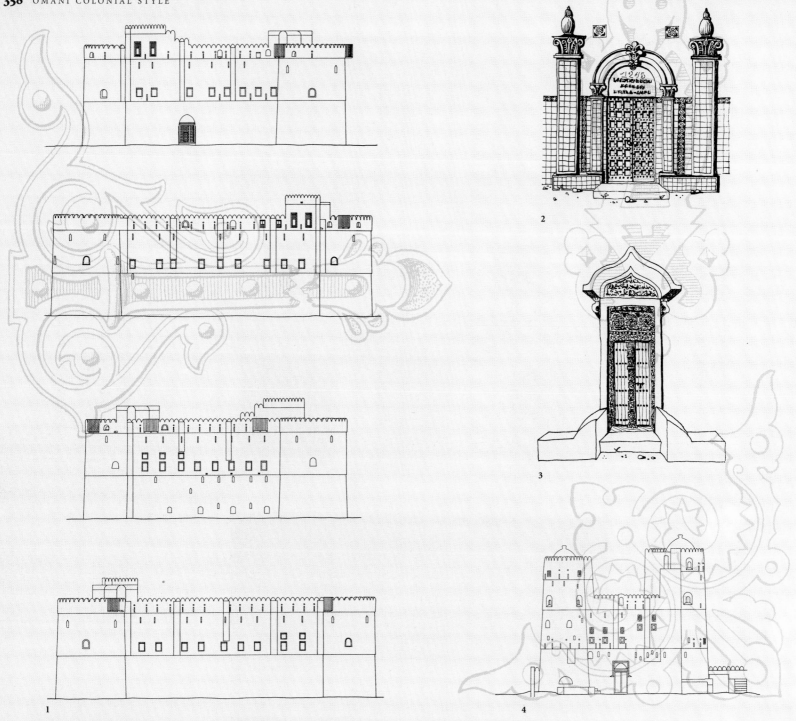

1

2

3

4

SCULPTED DOORS

When a house was built in an Omani colony, it was traditional for the doorway to be erected first. The power, wealth, and social status of the owner were represented by the dimensions of the house's entrance and the fineness and complexity of the inlay and carving used to decorate it. Such decorations included passages from the Koran and symbols intended to preserve the dwelling from ill fortune. Other motifs included waves, referring to the activities of merchants and navigators, and incense and date palms, symbolizing abundance and wealth. A number of designs predate Islam and represent lotus flowers, which may have been associated with Egyptian fertility symbols, and fish, which can be traced back to the Syrian goddess Atargatis or the golden fish of ancient Egypt.

Many of the doors are covered with brass studs. The custom presumably derived from a medieval Indian tradition, when such knobs were used to stop elephants from battering down doors. An Arab traveler who visited the island in 915 recorded that elephants abounded on the island, and Marco Polo made the same claim around 1295. Though they must have died out long before the Omanis arrived, the tradition had survived and the colonists took it over, if only for purely decorative reasons.

The oldest of the carved doorways dates from 1694 and is now the entrance to the National Museum in Stone Town. The many others scattered through the old quarter of the city are not as old but they are equally beautiful and richly decorated.

5

6

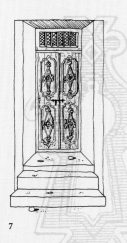

7

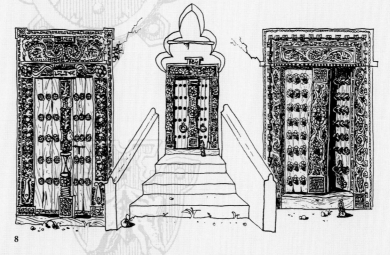

8

9

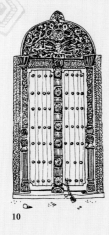

10

11

12

1. Elevations of Al Felaij, a typical Omani fort. The massive walls have few openings and give away nothing of the sumptuous rooms concealed behind. Only the inlaid wooden doors hint at the luxuries inside.

2. Door on an Omani colonial residence.

3. Door to an Omani-style house.

4. Bayt Na'man, an Omani fort.

5. Doorway set in a tympanum supported by pilasters. The composition recalls a temple.

6. Two pilasters topped by pinnacles framing a doorway surmounted by a curved tympanum.

7. A simple doorway with a few steps.

8. Two street-level doors surrounding a third set at the top of a flight of steps. The grouping is surmounted by a multifoil tympanum.

9. A simple door with a richly decorated frame.

10. Doorway in Stone Town topped by a round tympanum.

11. Mixtilinear tympanum over a doorway in Stone Town.

12. Stone Town doorway with a pointed tympanum.

Bibliography

General Studies

S. Calloway, E. Cromley. *The Elements of Style*. New York, 1996.

O. Guaita. *Segni di villa. L'eccellenza della dimora nel mondo*. Milan, 1998.

R. Luraghi. *Ascesa e tramonto del colonialismo*. Turin, 1964.

W. Markov. *Sommario di storia coloniale*. Milan, 1972.

K. M. Panikkar. *Storia della dominazione europea in Asia dal Cinquecento ai giorni nostri*. Turin, 1972.

C. Pavanati Bettoni. *Colonialismo*. Milan, 1997.

C. Pavanati Bettoni. *Le scoperte geografiche e l'espansione coloniale fino al secolo XVIII*. Milan, 1985.

Storia e imperi dell'Africa coloniale. Milan, 1986.

F. Surdich. *Esplorazioni geografiche e sviluppo del colonialismo nell'età della rivoluzione industriale*, Florence, 1980.

British Colonial Style

F. S. Aijazuddin. *Lahore: Illustrated Views of the 19th Century*. Ahmedabad, India, 1991.

F. Arvidsson, M. Mohsin. *Lahore*. Hong Kong, 1995.

A. Caemmerer. *The Houses of Key West*. Sarasota, Florida, 1992.

R. Delehanty, R. Sexton. *In the Victorian Style*. San Francisco, 1997.

M. Eichler de Saint Jorre, N. Ardill, C. Bossu-Picat. *Demeures d'Archipel. Seychelles*. Mahé, Seychelles, 1989.

M. Folsom. *Great American Mansions and Their Stories*. Mamaroneck, New York, 1963.

H. Fraser, R. Hughes. *Historic Houses of Barbados*. Barbados, 1986.

J. Fujii. *Under the Hula Moon: Living in Hawaii*. New York, 1992.

D. K. Gleason. *Virginia Plantation Homes*. Baton Rouge/London, 1989.

S. Guest, J. Harpur. *Private Gardens of Australia*. New York, 1990.

The Historic Houses of Australia. Sydney, 1988.

Historic New Zealand. Auckland, 1992.

L. Invernizzi Tettoni. *Myanmar Style: Art, Architecture and Design of Burma*. Hong Kong, 1998.

L. Invernizzi Tettoni, E. Ong. *Living in Sarawak*. London, 1996.

M. Lane. *Architecture of the Old South: Mississippi & Alabama*. New York, 1989.

Lee Kip Lin. *The Singapore House*. Singapore, 1988.

L. Linsley, J. Aron. *Key West Houses*. New York, 1992.

I. Macdonald-Smith, S. Shorto. *Bermuda Gardens & Houses*. New York, 1996.

D. McGill, G. Sheehan. *Landmarks: Notable Historic Buildings of New Zealand*, Auckland, 1997.

G. Michel, A. Martinelli. *I palazzi reali dell'India*. Milan, 1994.

M. Randall. *The Mansions of Long Island's Gold Coast*. New York, 1987.

R. Schezen, S. Johnston. *Palm Beach Houses*. New York, 1991.

R. Schezen, J. Mulvagh, M. A. Weber. *Newport Houses*. New York, 1989.

A. Spoule, M. Pollard. *The Country House Guide*. Boston, n.d.

Spanish Colonial Style

B. Barney, F. Ramírez. *La arquitectura de las casas de hacienda en la Valle del Alto Cauca*. Bogotá, 1994.

Caribbean Style. New York, 1985.

R. Carley, A. Brizzi. *Cuba: 400 Years of Architectural Heritage*. New York, 1997.

M. E. García Ugarte, J. M. Rivero Torres. *Esplendor y poderío de las haciendas queretanas*. Querétaro, Mexico, 1991.

G. Gasparini. *Casa venezolana*. Caracas, 1992.

L. Invernizzi Tettoni, T. Sosrowaroyo. *Filipino Style*. London, 1997.

W. Lunapkins. *La casa adobe*. Santa Fe, New Mexico, 1986.

R. Rendón Garcini. *Haciendas de México*. Mexico City, 1994.

J. Rigau. *Puerto Rico 1900: Turn-of-the-Century Architecture in the Hispanic Caribbean 1890–1930*. New York, 1992.

M. Sáenz Quesado, X. A. Verstraeten. *Estancias: The Great Houses and Ranches of Argentina*. New York, 1992.

S. and L. Seth. *Adobe: Houses and Interiors of Taos, Santa Fe and the Southwest*. Stamford, Connecticut, 1988.

T. Street-Porter. *Casa mexicana*. New York, 1989.

G. Tellez. *Casa colonial. Arquitectura doméstica neogranadina*. Bogotá, 1995.

French Colonial Style

J. Arrigo, D. Dietrich. *Louisiana's Plantation Homes: The Grace and Grandeur*. Stillwater, Minnesota, 1991.

F. Badets, D. Duteil. *Antilles et Réunion. Habitations coloniales*. Paris, 1989.

Caribbean Style. New York, 1985.

F. Gagnon Pratte. *Maisons de campagne des montréalais 1892–1924*. Montreal, 1987.

J. Gallotti. *Le jardin et la maison arabe en Maroc*. Paris, 1926.

N. Ghachem-Benkirane, R. Saharoff. *Marrakech. Demeures et jardins secrets*. Paris, 1990.

Maisons traditionnelles de l'Ile Maurice. N.p., 1990.

B. Marry, R. Suvélor, J. L. de Laguarigue. *Maisons des îles Martinique*. Le François, France, 1998.

C. Vaisse, C. Barat, Y. Augeard. *Cases créoles de l Réunion*. N.p., 1993.

J. Wesley Cooper. *Ante-Bellum Houses of Natchez* Natchez, Mississippi, 1983.

Portuguese Colonial Style

Fazendas. Solares da Região Cafeeira do Brasil Imperial Rio de Janeiro, 1990.

F. T. Fracoso Pires, N. Sapieha. *Fazendas: The Grea Houses and Plantations of Brazil*. New York, 1995.

Dutch Colonial Style

J. Guillermo, N. Sapieha. *Dutch Houses and Castles* London, 1990.

T. Hock Beng. *Tropical Architecture and Interiors Tradition-Based Design of Indonesia, Malaysia, Singapore Thailand*. Singapore, 1994.

D. Huijgers, L. Ezechiels. *Landhuizen van Curaçao en Bonaire*. Amsterdam, 1991.

L. Invernizzi Tettoni, W. Warren. *Balinese Gardens*. London, 1995.

S. Sosrowardoyo, P. Schoppert. *Java Style*. Singapore, 1997.

G. Viney. *Colonial Houses of South Africa*. Cape Town, 1988.

Ottoman Colonial Style

F. Davis. *The Palace of Topkapi in Istanbul*. New York, 1970. D. Kroyanker. *Gerusalemme, l'architettura*. Venice, 1994.

Chinese Colonial Style

Giardini cinesi classici. Milan, 1990.

M. Keswick. *The Chinese Garden*. London, 1978.

Korean Ancient Palaces. Seoul, 1988.

Italian Colonial Style

F. Amin, D. Willetts, A. Matheson. *Journey through Ethiopia*. Nairobi, 1997.

Apolloni, Zagnoni, Cresleri. *Architettura nelle colonie italiane in Africa*. Bologna, n.d.

Architettura italiana d'Oltremare 1870–1940. Venice, 1993.

Omani Colonial Style

M. A. Bianciifiori. *Biancifiori: Works of Architectura Restoration in Oman*. Rome, 1994.

W. Dinteman. *Forts of Oman*. Dubai, 1993.

S. Kay, D. Zandi. *Architectural Heritage of the Gulf*. Dubai, 1991.